GIVING TO THE GIVER: WORSHIP THAT PLEASES GOD

GIVING
TO THE
GIVER

Worship that Pleases God

RANDY PETERSEN

Tyndale House Publishers, Inc.
Wheaton, Illinois

Scripture quotations, unless otherwise noted, are
from the *Holy Bible,* New International Version.
Copyright © 1973, 1978, 1984 International Bible
Society. Used by permission of Zondervan Bible
Publishers. Quotations marked NKJV are taken
from the *Holy Bible,* New King James Version.
Copyright © 1979, 1980, 1982, Thomas Nelson
Inc., Publishers. Quotations marked KJV are from
the Authorized King James Version.

Library of Congress Catalog Card Number 90-61233
ISBN 0-8423-0415-0
Copyright © 1990 by Randy Petersen
All rights reserved
Printed in the United States of America

95 94 93 92 91 90
9   8   7   6   5   4   3   2   1

To my brother Ken
who woke me up to worship

CONTENTS

ACKNOWLEDGMENTS

Somebody smart once said that scholars write books at the beginning of their careers and at the end. The young ones think they know everything, and the old ones do. I'm hardly a scholar, just an observer, but readers should still be glad I didn't write this book ten years ago, when I first wanted to.

Fresh out of college, I thought I knew everything then. This decade has mellowed some of my thinking and ripened it. A number of people have helped in this ripening process. They deserve mention here.

My family has supported and sharpened my ideas. Mom and Dad have been a valuable sounding board, and sister Kathy has been a constant spur to my creativity. But brother Ken gets the dedication of this book because he was there at the start of my worship interest, showing me by example and keen analysis what worship meant.

Jim Young, my theater professor, helped start the stirrings of worship in me with a course called "Church and Theater." And though he doesn't know it, Bob Webber's "History and Theology of Worship" opened a treasure chest of ideas that I'm still unpacking.

Bill and Linda Richardson and the First Baptist Church of Glen Ellyn, Illinois, helped me put some of my ideas into practice. They also taught me much. This book is half theirs.

David Mains has inspired me with a sense of Christ's presence in my life, the very heart of worship. Parts of this book belong to Al Berg, Jana Redlich, Jana Childers, Katherine Gonzalez, and Joel Mac-Donald, whether they know it or not. Seeds they planted grew into chapters of this book. I pray that this book may plant seeds of worship in the lives of you readers.

"May the God of peace, who through the blood of the eternal covenant brought back from the dead our Lord Jesus, that great Shepherd of the sheep, equip you with everything good for doing his will, and may he work in us what is pleasing to him, through Jesus Christ, to whom be glory for ever and ever. Amen" (Heb. 13:20-21).

ONE
THE VACUUM IN OUR HEARTS

People need to worship. Deep in the human heart is the awareness that this is what we were meant to do. Even when we try to ignore them, the voices come to us: Give, yield, kneel . . . to someone, something . . . higher, better, beyond.

It has been called a "God-shaped vacuum." People have tried to fill it with all sorts of gods: alive or dead; far away or deep inside; animal-like or humanoid; ideology, philosophy, pastime. Whatever god we choose, we feel compelled to kneel at its shrine.

After years of youthful struggle, Augustine prayed, "Our hearts are restless until they find their rest in thee." He had scurried from Manichaean mysticism to Neo-Platonic philosophy to Roman paganism. He had devoted himself to sex, to scholarship, to politics. Nothing filled that vacuum until he worshiped Christ.

Those wise old Presbyterians who compiled the Westminster Shorter Catechism said it well: "The chief end of man is to glorify God and to enjoy him forever." This is what we were made for. As A.W. Tozer put it, "God made us to be worshipers." When we are not worshiping our Creator we are like the lawn mower used to slice tomatoes; that is not what it was intended to do. It is likely to make a mess of things; perhaps it will break down. It will not be a happy machine.

"Without worship," Tozer said, "we go about miserable." Later he called worship "the normal employment of moral beings." So, when

1

we aren't worshiping our Creator, we feel . . . well, unemployed. We're the laid-off steelworker shuffling around the house, turning on the TV, turning it off, sitting down, then standing up again. What is there to do? The God-shaped vacuum yawns within us, as we long to find rest. We search for a god worthy of our worship. False gods promise to fill the void. They excite our passions for a time but leave us longing. We are restless until we fall in worship before the God who made us.

Oh, yeah? That may have been the case with Augustine and his cadre of fourth-century yuppies, but in modern times who worships? This is an age of disillusionment. Nothing, no one, no-how is worthy of worship. Worship is silly.

The compelling need to worship has been driven deeper, almost out of sight, out of mind. Moderns try to convince themselves that *they* are the measure of this world; there is no need to bow to anyone anymore. A generation ago we worshiped sports heroes, politicians, entertainers. Now the ballplayers take drugs, the politicians take bribes, and the entertainers mock themselves on talk shows. A generation ago we worshiped America, church, family. The modern consensus is that these institutions have lost our trust, forfeited our honor. It is silly to worship them. It is silly to worship at all.

Like most heresies, this is half true. We may have exalted heroes or institutions too much. And it *is* silly to worship a god that is not God. Remember that Elijah mocked the worshipers of Baal in downright bawdy terms. Through Isaiah, God himself made fun of those who carved idols out of dead wood and then bowed before them.

But the modern doctrine of nonworship has gone too far, ruling out expressions of worship for the true God. It is silly, so they say, to believe an ancient book bears divine words. It is silly to sit in pews and sing songs about a dead Jew. It is silly to take bread and wine in prayerful meditation. It is silly to kneel, to raise one's hands in joy, to be dunked under water. Unfortunately, these sentiments often show up in the church.

We keep trying to redefine what we do. We go to church to receive ethical or inspirational teaching, we say. We go to see our friends. We go to get a blessing from a religious experience. We go to enjoy the music of the choir. That's fine, say the moderns; whatever turns you on. Just keep control of yourself and don't do anything silly.

Underneath, deep inside the human soul, is still the passion for worship. It bubbles up sometimes, in moments of aesthetic delight, or when people are in love. It can be embarrassing, but it is generally seen as harmless. We quickly make fun of such expressions of worship and suppress them. Sometimes that inner passion for worship gets pressed into strange shapes: the current fascination with Eastern religions and mysticism, for instance. Even there, people try to play both games. They reorient their worship into a self-help mechanism. By and large, they don't give themselves to these new gods; they take from them what they need to satisfy their sense of the Beyond—then they move on to other mystic experiences.

In a way, we do the same thing in church. We dabble. We take more than we give. It's a cafeteria of spiritual delights. It's a petting zoo where we touch our Creator and go home. We certainly wouldn't want to get into the cage with him. That would be dangerous, a silly thing to do.

The Apostle Paul spoke of the gospel as foolishness. He dared the Corinthians to believe it because "the foolishness of God is wiser than men." Way back then, those Greek philosophers were already cooping up worship in the human mind, beginning to ignore the body and soul. The idea of a God who became a Jewish man and died a criminal's death—and rose physically from the dead!—well, it just didn't make sense. Paul agreed that it appeared as foolishness to human reason. But it was true. God works in strange ways.

Christians today need to take that dare. We need to give ourselves wholly to our Creator, believing in the astonishing truth he has revealed about Jesus Christ and expressing our devotion as he wants us to—no matter how "silly" it may appear to outsiders. God is the measure of our world, and we have worth only because of him.

From the very start, Christians were those who worshiped Jesus Christ. It was a world of worshipers back then—everybody worshiped some deity.

The Jews worshiped Yahweh and found it scandalous to worship this Jesus in addition to Yahweh. The Christians kept explaining that Jesus was the Almighty God, the promised Messiah. To worship the Son was the only true way to worship the Father.

Pluralism marked the Greek and Roman world. There was widespread toleration of religious beliefs. Some worshiped the traditional Roman gods, though increasingly these were bypassed in favor of cults from the East. Many worshiped Isis, or Mithra, or Dionysius, or Fortuna. Bring your Jesus along, they said, we can worship him, too. Jesus could easily join the committee of ruling deities. But the

Christians insisted that it couldn't work like that. Jesus demanded exclusive worship. He would not be a committee member; he was Lord. One could not worship Isis and Christ, or Apollo and Christ, or Caesar and Christ. It was Christ or nothing.

This obstinacy earned the wrath of Rome. For 250 years, with varying intensity, persecution went on. Worshiping Jesus could get you killed.

The world is safer these days for those who worship Jesus, at least in the Christianized West. The dangers are subtler. Our culture, like ancient Rome's, is pluralistic. Believe what you want. Live and let live. Worship whatever, but don't take it too seriously.

Our culture doesn't kill us for worshiping Jesus, though it may give us bad reviews. It is in very bad taste, they say, to insist that your beliefs are right and everyone else's are wrong. It is rude to foist your religion on someone else. And it is backward to let your beliefs dominate your life.

We don't like bad reviews, so we adjust. Not only do we try to make our worship seem less silly, we make it less offensive. We adapt to the beliefs of our culture. Though we still steer clear of false gods with recognizable names—Allah, Buddha, Shirley MacLaine—we subtly begin to worship Mammon, Erotica, or Fortuna. Our Christianity becomes less vital as we invite these onto the ruling committees of our lives.

What is the answer? It is not hard to figure out. We need to redefine ourselves as those who worship Jesus and only Jesus. But what is this thing called "worship," which marks people's souls and makes enemies? What is this subversive activity?

This book will help answer that question.

Worship is a big idea. It can mean many things. You may not like that. It might be a good idea to present a definition here at the outset. But a definition (by definition) limits an idea. When you say what worship is, you imply that it is not a hundred other things. Let us hold the door open for a while and welcome as many "definitions" as we can. Through the course of this book, we will sort through them and come to some conclusions.

To start with: Worship is an inner compulsion in the human soul. We know, somewhere within us, that there is an Other, a God to whom we must answer, to whom we owe something. God placed this awareness in us when he made us. Sin has tried to drown out this whisper of desire, and in some cases has succeeded, at least for a time. But the

4

longing to worship something remains within us: We need to give ourselves to the one who made us.

As such, worship is a *direction* more than anything. We direct ourselves toward our Creator, we attend to him, we give to him.

As we think about worship, in Scripture and in the church's history, we can begin to discern three levels of worship. If the early Christians, for instance, distinguished themselves by being worshipers of Christ, what did this look like? What was involved?

1. *Personal devotion to Jesus.* The ancient Roman might have prayed to Fortuna for good luck. The Christian communicated with God through Christ. And that still sets us apart. The Muslim prays to Allah, the Buddhist meditates on the teachings of Buddha, the Mammon-worshiper counts his money. But the Christian interacts on this personal level with Christ.

2. *Obedience.* Christians became known in the Roman Empire for their life-styles of love and morality. They obeyed Christ's teachings. This was what attracted people to Christianity in spite of the flare-ups of persecution. The Roman religions were generally devoid of moral teaching. The Romans did, however, require obedience to the laws of Rome and ordered residents of the empire to show their loyalty by worshiping the spirit of Caesar. This the Christ-worshipers refused to do.

Today worshipers of all kinds show their loyalties in their daily lives. The Buddhist not only meditates on Buddha's words but applies them to his life. The Muslim tries to win the world for Allah. The modern Fortuna-worshiper plays the lottery every morning. The money-lover compounds his investments.

The Christian worships Jesus by obeying him in showing love to others and in matters of personal holiness.

3. *Corporate commitment.* Devotees of the various religions of Rome would meet regularly with their groups to honor their gods. There were banquets, orgies, sacrifices, and other rituals. Many of these groups had elaborate temples where they held their meetings.

The Christians also met regularly together, usually in houses. They also shared meals, prayed together, sang together, and were instructed in the faith. Often under threat of arrest and death they met, but they met. That was an integral part of what it meant to be a Christian, to be a part of the Christian church, to meet for worship with other Christians.

And so today, even in an age of isolation, we see various temples in our cities. Less formal "worship" may go on at ballgames and rock

5

concerts. But Christians still worship Christ by joining with other Christians. Thus we signal our allegiance.

These three levels of worship come as a package. We need all three. Various portions of Scripture criticize God's people for imbalances. They sometimes ignored certain parts of the package—that had to be set right.

This book, as a balancing action, will emphasize level three, corporate worship. Evangelicalism has been good at emphasizing personal devotion and obedience, but many of us don't quite know what to do when we come together for worship. Thus this book will examine scriptural principles and strategies for the church as a whole. However, that impulse for worship occurs on all three levels, and we can never—and should never—completely separate them.

With that as our starting block, let's race through Scripture. What does the Bible say about this thing called worship? It uses various words in Hebrew and Greek, each with different nuances. It gives us examples of God's people at worship—and others worshiping their gods. What can we learn?

Let us continue to amass data before trying to prove any points. Oh, there are some wonderful conclusions to be drawn from all this, and we'll get to them. But for now, let's take a brief tour of Scripture, beginning with the New Testament, and see what is there.

TWO
DIGGING FOR
MEANING
(MATTHEW 2, 4)

You're an archaeologist, slaving away at some Mideast mound of earth, picking through the past for something intelligible. Suddenly you notice something at your feet. You dig it out—it's a clay tablet. You carefully note its location and then try to decipher the strange markings on it.

In the succeeding days, you and your team uncover thousands of these tablets. You've stumbled upon an ancient library. But what do the markings mean?

You call in a paleolinguist to crack the code. The expert has his methods. He looks for patterns in the symbols, structures that might be words, similarities with other languages of the region. He begins to make some educated guesses, but you're still far from translation.

Then one day you dig up another tablet, only this one has, alongside the strange scratchings, some letters that you recognize. It's Greek to you—but of course you have studied Greek, so you know it well. And there's some Hebrew. An ancient scholar apparently translated this tablet into Greek and Hebrew. Here is the "Rosetta Stone" the paleolinguist has needed. Now he has the key to unlock the archaic language.

But still the expert comes across a word he doesn't know. *Zilf*, let's say. The Rosetta Stone doesn't have it. There are no parallels with any Hebrew or Arabic words. Yet it shows up here, and here, and here, in the excavated tablets.

What to do? Look for internal clues. Context. As he examines its uses, the expert finds that "zilfing" seems to be something people do. One man zilfs corn. Does he grow it, harvest it, plant it, eat it, or pop it? Another woman zilfs bread. Maybe it means to bake, to prepare for eating. But then we read of a family sitting down to zilf dinner. "Eat" seems to be the best translation. But wait—another tablet tells of someone zilfing water. So it is more than eating; it is consuming. But, in another text, a fire zilfs a forest and, in another, the ocean zilfs a small boat. So it has a metaphorical sense as well.

Taken together, in context, the uses of the word give the whole picture. The paleolinguist ferrets out the full meaning of the word, and it is more than one English word can translate. "Consume" probably comes closest, but the meaning even goes beyond that.

Biblical words can be like that. We often forget this as we read Scripture. We think we know what *redemption* means, or *grace*, or *holy*. But we forget that these words, as we know them, are merely the English words that come closest to the original Greek or Hebrew words. The original biblical message came in a different culture, a different time, a different language—and the words often carry pieces of their cultures within them.

I don't mean to say that we English speakers can't know the biblical message. I'm not saying that you have to read Greek and Hebrew to be a first-class Christian. Translators have done a great job of putting Scripture into our words. And preachers and commentators are good at giving us the nuances behind the words. We just need to keep those nuances in mind. We need to fill out the English words we read with the meanings we glean from their biblical contexts.

Thus *redemption* should call to mind the story of Boaz *redeeming* Ruth and marrying her. *Grace* should speak to us of gift-giving. *Holy* should remind us of Isaiah before God's throne, his lips cleansed by the burning coal. Wherever we read these words in Scripture, we should fill out their meanings with these pictures, and others.

Worship is such a word, one that deserves special attention. Our English word has a rich history, harking back to "worth-ship." *Worship*, in English, means to declare or recognize the worth of something or someone. But, as wonderful as the English word is, it hardly begins to tap the reservoir of meaning in the biblical words it translates. No question about it: Worth-ship is a great way to look at biblical worship. One thinks of the song in Revelation: "Worthy is the Lamb, who was slain" (Rev. 5:12). But let us not stop there. Let us dig for more of what

8

Scripture tells us about worship. Let's allow the Bible to define this word for us.

In a way, we are playing the "zilf" game here. We are unearthing clay tablets and looking for clues. So let us start from scratch. Pretend you have never heard the word *worship*. Pretend you know nothing about it. We'll take notes on its meaning directly from Scripture.

The Greek word we'll trace first is *proskuneo,* the most common word for "worship." We don't have to go far in the New Testament to find it: Matthew chapter 2, the familiar story of the magi.

> After Jesus was born in Bethlehem in Judea, during the time of King Herod, Magi from the east came to Jerusalem and asked, "Where is the one who has been born king of the Jews? We saw his star in the east and have come to worship him." (Matt. 2:1-2)

After King Herod consulted with his priests and directed the wise men to Bethlehem, he asked the magi to return and tell him where the child was, "so that I too may go and worship him" (v. 8). We learn later that Herod had no such intention; he wanted to kill the child. But the wise men go on to Bethlehem.

> On coming to the house, they saw the child with his mother Mary, and they bowed down and worshiped him. Then they opened their treasures and presented him with gifts of gold and of incense and of myrrh. (Matt. 2:11)

What do we learn about "worship" from its three uses in this passage?

1. Worship is something you do to a king, even if the king is a child and even if you are a king yourself. When the magi announced their intentions, Herod was disturbed, but not because it was unusual or inappropriate to worship a child. He was disturbed because any newborn king would be a threat to his own reign. He masked his displeasure with a creative lie. He pretended to be willing to worship the child himself. Apparently the wise men saw nothing strange in this.

2. Worship is something these magi came a long way to do. We learn in verse 16 that Jesus may have been two years old by the time the wise men showed up. That means that they may have been traveling (or preparing to travel) for two years. They must have considered the worship of this youngster a high priority.

3. Worship was something the wise men needed to be there to do. That is, long-distance worship was not an option for them. They traveled a long way because, as far as they were concerned, their presence was required.

4. Worship is associated with bowing down. We will see this frequently in the Gospels.

5. Worship, in this case, is accompanied by gift-giving. We don't know yet whether gift-giving has to accompany worship, but it is worth noting that it was all part of the magi's actions—bowing, worshiping, giving. Note also that these were substantial gifts. The wise men didn't run out to get a necktie or something on sale. They gave expensive presents.

The next use of *proskuneo* occurs a few chapters later, in another fairly familiar story, the temptation of Jesus. In the desert, Jesus fasted for forty days, then the devil came and tempted him to turn stones into bread. Quoting Scripture, Jesus resisted the temptation. The devil then urged Jesus to jump from the highest point of the Temple. Again, quoting Scripture, Jesus refused. Finally, the devil took Jesus to a high mountain and showed him all the kingdoms of the world and their splendor.

> "All this I will give you," he said, "if you will bow down and worship me." Jesus said to him, "Away from me, Satan! For it is written: 'Worship the Lord your God, and serve him only.'" (Matt. 4:8-10)

What further clues about "worship" can we pick up here?

1. It is desirable to be worshiped. The devil wants worship—and he is willing to pay for it. The Lord also wants worship—exclusive worship. And he refuses to give that up even for all the kingdoms of the world.

2. Again, worship is associated with bowing down. It seems to be a package deal: bow down and worship. That is what Satan wants. That is what Jesus refused to do. Jesus didn't bargain. He did not say, "Look, I'll bow down, but I won't worship, so why don't you give me half the kingdoms of the world and an option on the splendor." No, the two are obviously tied together.

3. The Lord God is the only proper recipient of worship. We see here how very, very important this fact is.

10

Stop and think about it for a minute. Satan is offering all the kingdoms of the world. Some commentators have questioned whether these kingdoms were really his to give. But the Bible does speak of the devil as "the prince of this world" (John 12:31; 14:30; 16:11; see also 2 Cor. 4:4). Since the fall of Adam and Eve, Satan has become, in a sense, the ruler of the world and its systems.

God desperately wants his people back, so he devises his plan. He will send his Son to earth. The Son will die, taking on himself the penalty for sin, and rise from death, releasing the people of the world from Satan's control. As Jesus, the Son, debates with the devil in the desert, a great amount of pain and struggle lies ahead of him. The plan calls for him to be alienated from his Father at the point of his death, to bear the weight of the world's sin.

But wait, Satan said. "Why bother? I'll give you your people back. Just bow down and worship me. No need to go through all that pain, Jesus. Take the easy way out. Worship me."

The devil's no dummy. He knows how badly God wants the world, how dearly he loves it. And so he holds it out as bait. "It's yours, Jesus. I'll take a hike. No more tempting. No more wickedness. Do all the righteous things you want with it. I'm out of the picture. All you have to do is bow down. It's simple. Just worship me."

But as much as God longs for the world, there is one thing more important—exclusive worship from its people. It wouldn't mean much to have all the kingdoms of the world if he couldn't have their worship. And that would be the situation if the Son of God were to bow before the tempter.

I remember playing the "wish" game as a child. A friend and I were mulling over what we would ask for if some genie granted us each one wish. "I'd wish for all the money in the world," my friend said, and waited to see if I could top that. "Well," I said, "I'd wish for all the power in the world—and then I'd make you give me all your money."

That is the same sort of game Satan was trying to sucker Jesus into playing. If God had to give up his own preeminence, to share worship with the devil, all those kingdoms wouldn't be worth much. That is how important worship is.

Before we leave the temptation story, there are two more clues to dig out. Both have to do with the Old Testament verse quoted by Jesus. Here we have our Rosetta Stone, a cross-translation with a Hebrew text. And we find some fascinating things as we compare the two.

Jesus quoted Deuteronomy 6:13, with one minor change. Deuteronomy says: "Fear the LORD your God, serve him only and take your oaths in his name."

But Jesus, responding to Satan's temptation to "worship" him, substitutes *worship* for *fear*. These are not just tricks of English translation. The Septuagint, the Greek translation of the Old Testament used in Jesus' day, uses the Greek word for "fear," *phobeo,* in the Deuteronomy text. Jesus, as recorded by Matthew and also by Luke (4:8), clearly changes it to *proskuneo,* "worship." So we can make yet another observation from this text:

4. Jesus equated worship with fear. He was not really misquoting the Old Testament text; he was filling out its meaning. In that context, for the devil and for Jesus, fearing the Lord would keep one from worshiping anyone but the Lord.

The Deuteronomy passage has to do with idolatry and obedience. The following verses say: "Do not follow other gods, the gods of the peoples around you; for the LORD your God, who is among you, is a jealous God, and his anger will burn against you" (Deut. 6:14-15).

This, of course, is the essence of the first of the Ten Commandments: "You shall have no other gods before me" (Exod. 20:3). The Israelites were continually tempted to follow the religions of the surrounding nations. Fear of Jehovah would keep them from going astray.

"Fear," as it is used throughout the Old Testament, has positive and negative aspects. The fear of the Lord can mean "reverential awe," as many commentators have said. It can mean "healthy respect." But don't sell it short. It basically means being scared out of your wits.

We need to see this against the backdrop of competing religions. God often wooed his people with loving words, but so did others. The false prophets of other religions would sweet-talk the people into sampling their wares. There were sex religions and nature religions that promised good times and bountiful crops. What set the true God apart from them was that he had power and they didn't.

Nowadays we see power most blatantly at work in political campaigns. The major candidates come around to the local politicos, seeking support. The shrewd locals don't necessarily throw their influence toward the best candidate; they support the one they think will win. The winner, once elected, will have power. He will reward the many who helped him into office and shun those who opposed him. He has the power to make or break political careers. So, savvy low-level politicians often choose a candidate to support, not because they love the candidate's policies, but because they fear the consequences of not backing him.

The God of the Israelites was to be feared—and loved—because he was a real God. He had real power, unlike the other gods competing for his people's attention. He often used that power to shower blessings on his people, but they usually attributed his blessings to Baal or some other false deity. God expresses his frustration through the prophet Hosea: "She [Israel] has not acknowledged that I was the one who gave her the grain, the new wine and oil, who lavished on her the silver and gold—which they used for Baal" (Hos. 2:8).

Hosea went on to say that God would remove those blessings and be harsh with his people. If the loving expression of his power did not elicit loving obedience from Israel, perhaps the judging expression of his power would elicit fearful obedience. Either way, God will be obeyed.

In Proverbs we find the maxim: "The fear of the LORD is the beginning of knowledge" (Prov. 1:7, KJV). Perhaps it is the beginning because it is easier to learn fear than love. Perhaps as we grow in wisdom we learn to appreciate the loving power of God and love him back by obeying him. Perhaps we mature from fear into worship. And perhaps Jesus was expressing this progression as he subtly changed the translation of Deuteronomy 6:13.

That is conjecture. But we do know that worship is strongly associated with the fear of the Lord. We also know that the fear of the Lord involves three aspects: (1) recognition of God's reality and power (as opposed to the unreality and weakness of other gods); (2) recognition of the fact that God responds to what we do; (3) decision to obey his commands.

We see more about this obedience in yet another literary clue we cull from that Matthew-Deuteronomy connection.

5. Worship is associated with service. "Worship the Lord . . . and serve him only." These are not two unrelated commands. The way Jesus put them together, with a hint of Hebrew parallelism, may make them nearly synonymous.

What does it mean to serve God? Scripture speaks of service in two ways. One is just plain obedience. We serve God by doing what he says, as a servant would carry out the orders of his master. But service also refers to specific religious acts—going to temple to participate in the ceremonies. The psalmist used "serve the LORD with gladness" in

13

a parallel construction with "come before his presence with singing" (100:2, KJV). It is obviously a temple-going psalm, beginning with "Enter his gates with thanksgiving and his courts with praise." The Lord is present in his holy temple, so to come before his presence, in the Psalms, is to go to temple. To serve him is to perform the prescribed sacrifices. Contrarily, to serve other gods is to participate in their rituals, which are expressly forbidden to God's people, since, as Jesus put it later, "No one can serve two masters" (Matt. 6:24).

Note then the dual nature of service: everyday life and religious ceremonies. Might "worship" have the same duality? Note also that service means work. A servant is a worker. Even the performing of religious sacrifices was hard work for the Israelites. That may also teach us something about worship.

Let us pause a moment to review the clues we have gathered from just these two "clay tablets"—Matthew 2 and Matthew 4. We have been looking for nuances, associations, ideas. Here is what we have found:

Worship is due kings.

Worship is worth traveling for.

Worship sometimes requires being there. ("Come before his presence . . ." as well as the magi's journey.)

Worship is associated with bowing down.

Worship sometimes involves gift-giving.

Worship is desired very, very much by both the devil and God. It is worth more than the world's kingdoms.

We must worship God alone.

Worship involves the fear of God, which involves recognizing his power and obeying his commands.

Worship is related to service, both in everyday obedience and in special religious observance.

THREE
BOWING AND BELIEVING
(THE GOSPELS)

A murder has been committed. Quickly, Sherlock Holmes, Hercule Poirot, or Cagney and Lacey go to the scene of the crime. They are detectives, gathering evidence. Some threads on the carpet. A strange scent in the air. A footprint in the flower garden. Oh, it may be nothing, but they gather it all, write it all down, in the hope that one of these details will help catch the killer.

They are trying to define the killer's identity, much as we are trying to define *worship*. We are gathering evidence, hoping to see certain patterns emerge. Some clues may not amount to much, but we must observe everything.

As we continue to track *proskuneo,* this Greek word for "worship," through the Gospels, a pattern begins to emerge.

> And behold, a leper came and worshiped Him [Jesus], saying, "Lord, if You are willing, You can make me clean." (Matt. 8:2, NKJV)

> While He spoke these things to them, behold, a ruler came and worshiped Him, saying, "My daughter has just died, but come and lay Your hand on her and she will live." (Matt. 9:18, NKJV)

> Then she [a woman of Canaan] came and worshiped Him, saying, "Lord, help me!" (Matt. 15:25, NKJV)

15

> Then came to him the mother of Zebedee's children with her sons, worshiping him, and desiring a certain thing of him. And he said unto her, "What wilt thou?" She saith unto him, "Grant that these my two sons may sit, the one on thy right hand, and the other on the left, in thy kingdom." (Matt. 20:20, KJV)

> But when he [the demon-possessed man] saw Jesus from afar, he ran and worshiped Him. And he cried out with a loud voice and said, "What have I to do with You, Jesus, Son of the Most High God? I implore You by God that You do not torment me." (Mark 5:6-7, NKJV)

It seems to be the thing to do, when approaching Jesus—to "worship" him. But what does it mean in these verses—"came and worshiped," "ran and worshiped"? Literally, it means they bowed down or knelt down before him. In fact, I used other translations for these verses because the New International Version doesn't use *worship* for *proskuneo* here. In each case, the NIV has "knelt down."

There is a good reason for that. *Proskuneo* comes from two earlier Greek words. *Pros* is a prefix meaning "before, in front of." We have the prefix "pro" in many English words. A prologue is the part of a book that comes before the rest of it. A program is something written that you hold in front of you as you watch a ball game or opera. A professor stands in front of a class and "professes," or declares things.

Kuneo comes from the verb "to kiss." Now *pros-kuneo,* to kiss-in-front-of, is not any romantic interaction. It refers to kissing the feet of a superior. This was an ancient custom. A servant would prostrate himself before his master, lying flat on the ground, and await his orders. Later, the custom became more stylized (and a bit less dirty). As a symbol of respect, one would kneel before a superior. This is, no doubt, what the people were doing in the verses quoted above. The New International Version has it right: they knelt before Jesus.

So we see something very important about worship here—its physical aspect. The wise men bowed down to worship the Christ-child. The devil urged Jesus to bow down and worship him. And numerous people came up to Jesus during his ministry and knelt before him. Whatever else *worship* means, it at least has a strong physical sense to it.

16

But what else can it mean? We have divided up the word, *proskuneo,* in the original Greek. Shouldn't that settle it? Isn't that, then, the definition of this word?

Not entirely. Words evolve in meaning from literal to figurative. We are metaphorical people. We delight in taking concrete, physical terms and applying them to abstract situations. In that way concrete words take on abstract meanings.

We see this most clearly in our figures of speech. I've been pounding my head against a wall trying to think of examples. Oh, there's one there. I haven't really been pounding the wall, of course. That merely expresses an abstraction—my frustration—in concrete terms. And maybe it shed new light on the subject for you. Figurative light, of course. I'm not shining a flashlight over your shoulder as you read.

Some words or phrases are further along in this "evolutionary process." If someone is "railroaded," we hardly think of trains. When you cater to somebody, you don't serve him food—in fact, we seldom consider that meaning. Perhaps when someone first coined the term "landslide victory" in an election, it called to mind plummeting rocks, but not anymore.

So it is with *proskuneo,* worship. We have a literal, concrete meaning: bowing down. But it carries huge spiritual meaning as well. It developed through the ages from the physical act to the spirit behind the physical act. In Scripture we see both.

When the ruler, the leper, and others were kneeling down before Jesus, it was not merely a physical action. It was not as if they slipped and fell at his feet. Each of them had decided to kneel before Jesus to express something spiritual—respect, honor. The word *proskuneo* in these verses does not just mean "kneeling down," as you might guess from the New International Version translation. Nor does it mean only "saying respectful things about someone," as you might guess from the King James Version and our modern assumptions of what "worship" is. It means "kneeling before a superior as an expression of worship (whatever that is)." The NIV translation works only if we understand this spiritual significance of kneeling.

Remember this point (we will deal with it more deeply later): Whatever else worship may involve, it has a strong physical sense to it. Yet it is not just a physical action. It is a physical expression of a spiritual commitment.

17

Now let us get back to that collection of verses in which people are falling at Jesus' feet. What else can we learn from them? Are there other unifying threads?

All of these people were asking favors. The leper wanted cleansing; the ruler wanted his daughter healed; the Canaanite woman wanted a demon exorcised from her daughter; Mrs. Zebedee wanted cabinet positions in Jesus' government for her sons; and the demons in the possessed man wanted mercy. They came; they knelt; they begged.

We don't often think of worship as favor-asking, but that is exactly what we see here. Think about it. What is involved in asking a favor?

Say I ask my brother to lend me ten dollars until payday. What is happening there? First, I'm assuming he has ten dollars to lend. Second, I am hoping that our relationship is so strong that he will want to. And third, I am placing myself in his debt.

It is the same undercurrent with the leper, the ruler, and the others. First, they recognize the power of Jesus to meet their needs. They are not going to every rabbi on the street, saying, "Heal me, please." They have presumably seen power in Jesus—and they believe he can help them. As the leper said, "If you want to, you can make me clean."

Second, they are hoping that Jesus will have compassion on them. Of these five, only Zebedee's wife might have had any previous interaction with Jesus; the others were strangers. And yet they hoped that Jesus' love would compel him to meet their needs. Thus they were trusting not only in his ability to help, but in his desire to help—not only in his power, but in his love.

Third, by the act of kneeling, they were putting themselves in subservience to Jesus. They were identifying themselves as people in need and identifying Jesus as the one they needed. This is perhaps the most difficult step. That is the very thing that might prevent me from asking my brother for a loan. My pride might keep me from admitting my need. But these people shook off their pride, knelt before Jesus, and begged for his help.

In a way, this is the flip side of fear, as we saw it in the last chapter. The fear of the Lord involves (1) recognizing his power; (2) recognizing that he cares what we do and responds to it, that there is some sort of a personal connection between him and us; and (3) committing ourselves to do what he says, putting ourselves in the role of obedient servant.

The favor-asking worship of Jesus, as we see it in these five snippets of Scripture, involves (1) recognizing his power; (2) trusting that he cares enough about us to want to help; and (3) making ourselves subservient.

So we see worship as a progression of sorts from the Old Testament theme of "the fear of the Lord." We recognize not only God's power, but also his love, and we respond accordingly. That may mean asking for help.

Consider the word *Hosanna*. Here is another interesting case of word evolution. You remember it as the cry of the crowd as Jesus rode into Jerusalem on Palm Sunday. It is a cry of praise. But the word originally meant, "Lord, save us!" It was a request, a cry for help.

It became a word of praise because it is the sort of thing you would say to someone strong enough to save you, a conquering king, perhaps, who would rout the Roman oppressors and restore the fortunes of Israel. So as Jesus entered Jerusalem in triumph, the people lifted their call for help and their cry of praise in the same word (even though they may not have been thinking of the word's history). "Lord, save us. You are mighty enough to do so." Worship, in that case, was both a declaration of the Lord's might and, embedded in the word *Hosanna*, a plea for divine aid.

We find another nugget of worship in the story of Peter's walk on water. The disciples, you remember, were boating across the Sea of Galilee when a storm came up. They saw Jesus walking toward them on the water, and they were afraid. Peter, at Jesus' invitation, walked out on the water to meet him.

> But when he saw the wind, he was afraid and, beginning to sink, cried out, "Lord, save me!" Immediately Jesus reached out his hand and caught him. "You of little faith," he said, "why did you doubt?" And when they climbed into the boat, the wind died down. Then those who were in the boat worshiped him, saying, "Truly you are the Son of God." (Matt. 14:30-33)

It is a story of faith and fear. When the disciples first saw Jesus, they thought he was a ghost, and they were terrified. Peter showed more faith than any of them when he stepped out on the raging water. Then he became afraid again—of the wind, of the storm, of falling, of drowning in the sea—and he started to sink. But then he showed faith enough to cry, "Lord, save me!" He was not thinking *Hosanna* at this point, but he trusted that Jesus could pull him out of danger.

19

Jesus then scolded Peter for his lack of faith. "Why did you doubt?" Perhaps Jesus was disappointed that the germ of faith that got Peter out on the waves to begin with didn't last. Peter showed promise of trusting Jesus completely, but he failed at the last moment.

In this context of faith and doubt, after the wind died down, the disciples worshiped Jesus. How? No doubt they were kneeling down before him. But what was going on spiritually? They acknowledged who he was: the Son of God. We find two more threads of evidence here. (1) Worship involves acknowledging the Lord's identity. (2) Worship, in this case, comes out of a situation in which both faith and doubt were expressed.

We see faith and identity again in John 9:38, at the conclusion of one of Scripture's most entertaining chapters. Jesus heals a man who had been born blind and, for a change, the Gospel-writer keeps the focus on the person healed, rather than following Jesus to his next miracle. First, the neighbors didn't believe he was the same beggar. Then the Pharisees sent in their team of special investigators. The man's parents coyly refused to back up their son's story, and the Pharisees continued to grill the beggar—who ended up chastising the Pharisees for their ignorance. All the while, a curious thing was happening to the man. At first, he didn't know much about this Jesus who healed him, but, as he was interrogated, he realized the miraculous proportions of what had happened. "If this man were not from God," he said, "he could do nothing." But the Pharisees remained blind to the evidence.

Then Jesus showed up, after the man had been excommunicated from the synagogue. He asked "Do you believe in the Son of Man?" This was, of course, the term Jesus borrowed from the Book of Daniel for himself, a reference to the Messiah who would come in glory to redeem Israel.

The blind man had never seen his healer. Jesus looked like just another man to him. "Who is he, sir?" the man asked. "Tell me so that I may believe in him."

Jesus said, "You have now seen him; in fact, he is the one speaking with you."

The man said, "Lord, I believe," and he worshiped Jesus (John 9:35-38).

Here we see that worship involves recognizing that Jesus is who he says he is, the Son of Man, and declaring that belief. We should note that "believing" here is more than just agreeing to the facts, though it includes that. The man wanted to believe in the Son of Man. In John's Gospel, that means committing oneself, trusting in the power of Jesus to deliver. (This is another great example of words that become richer in meaning.) It isn't really an issue of "head-belief versus heart-belief." For John the two go together. If you really accept the facts mentally—that Jesus was the Son of God—then you must commit yourself to him. The problem in John's day was not lack of commitment but lack of belief. False teachers were putting out false statements of who Jesus was. John made no secret of the fact that he wrote his Gospel "that you may believe that Jesus is the Christ, the Son of God, and that by believing you may have life in his name" (John 20:31). Believing is trusting, and that leads to life.

But we find a strange phrase at the end of Matthew's Gospel: "Then the eleven disciples went to Galilee, to the mountain where Jesus had told them to go. When they saw him, they worshiped him; but some doubted" (Matt. 28:16-17).

It was after the Resurrection. The disciples were reunited with their master. Worship was a natural response toward someone who had just conquered death. But some doubted.

The language of this verse is similar to that of the walking-on-water story. The disciples, during their three-year stint with Jesus, showed both doubt and faith. Peter was the prime example of that. He made a stirring profession of the lordship of Jesus, and, verses later, he tried to keep Jesus from going to Jerusalem to die. "Blessed are you," Jesus said to him and, verses later, "Get behind me, Satan!" (Matt. 16:13-23).

When Jesus chastised the disciples (and Peter) for their lack of faith (Matt. 14:31; 16:8), he didn't call them "faithless ones" (*apistes*), but "you of little faith" (*oligopistes*). There is some faith here, though not a lot—yet even a mustard seed's worth can move mountains (Matt. 17:20).

The disciples were on a journey, growing in faith as they learned from Jesus. Even as Jesus left them, some still doubted, but the Holy Spirit would continue to teach them. Thomas needed to see Jesus, to touch him, before he believed in the Resurrection. But he grew in faith through that experience. (That, by the way, is where Jesus used the word *faithless, apistis.* "Don't be faithless," he told Thomas, "but believing" (John 20:27). The disciples on the road to Emmaus seemed ignorant or doubtful regarding what Jesus had foretold about his resurrection, but he taught them and they believed. And here in Matthew's last chapter, Jesus met the disciples, they worshiped (and doubted), and then Jesus taught them. It is the word of Christ that conquers doubt.

We find worship in two other post-Resurrection appearances of Jesus. In Matthew 28, Mary Magdalene and "the other Mary" saw angels at Jesus' tomb. The angels announced the Resurrection. So the women hurried away from the tomb, "afraid yet filled with joy," and ran to tell the disciples. Suddenly Jesus met them and greeted them. They approached him, clasped his feet, and worshiped him. Jesus said, "Do not be afraid. Go and tell my brothers to go to Galilee . . ." (Matt. 28:1-10).

Note the physicality of the worship here. The women obviously threw themselves at Jesus' feet. They clasped his feet, perhaps not only to worship but to make sure he was real. (These were the feet one Mary had washed.) From Jesus' comment, we know they were afraid, but the text says joy was mingled with that fear. That is a strange combination, but a good one. Perhaps joy is the element we need to counterbalance the fear of Old Testament worship.

We see joy again at the end of Luke, at Jesus' ascension.

> While he was blessing them, he left them and was taken up into heaven. Then they worshiped him and returned to Jerusalem with great joy. And they stayed continually at the temple, praising God. (Luke 24:51-53)

For the first time, we see Jesus being worshiped in his absence. He was taken away from them, physically, and they needed to learn new ways of falling at his feet. Luke picked up this theme in his sequel, the Book of Acts. There we see the fledgling church at worship. Notice the immediate reference to the temple. That was where Jews worshiped God. It was only logical that the Son of God, once his bodily temple was removed from the scene, would be worshiped in the Jerusalem temple as well. And the early chapters of Acts show us that the church continued to worship daily at the temple.

This Luke 24 passage is an extension of the worship service that started in Matthew 28:16. There we saw the disciples in Galilee, worshiping Jesus and doubting. But now we have had forty days of teaching by Jesus, starting with the Great Commission of Matthew 28:19-20 and ending with a similar Great Commission in Luke 24:46-49. At Jesus' words, their doubt turned to joy. Shouldn't the proclamation of God's Word in our worship services have the same effect?

As we sum up some of the threads of evidence we have gathered in this chapter, remember that we are not fully defining worship yet. We are still searching for clues, associations, hints.

1. Worship has a strong physical sense to it: bowing or kneeling down before someone. But this is not only physical. It is the bodily expression of a spiritual commitment.

2. Worship, in many Gospel accounts, involves asking favors. This includes a recognition of God's power, a hope in his compassion, and placing oneself in his debt.

3. Worship involves recognizing Jesus' identity.

4. This recognition can come out in strong statements of faith, but on occasion there is doubt as well. This doubt is generally dispelled by Christ's teaching.

5. Worship involves both fear and joy.

FOUR
DUST IN THE WIND
(JOHN 4)

Under the scorching Samarian sun, traveling the mountain ridge route from Judea to Galilee, Jesus stopped by the well outside the village of Sychar and sent his disciples into town to buy food.

It was hardly the place for a treatise on the theology of worship. And the woman coming to draw water—well, you wouldn't choose her as a debating partner. But there, by the well, with the woman, we learn the best news yet about worship.

The woman was just trying to escape from an embarrassing conversation. It had started simply enough. This stranger was sitting by the well as she came to draw water. Poor fellow, he was so thirsty, but he had no bucket to lower to the cool water below. He looked Jewish, though, so he would pay no attention to her, a Samaritan. Those Jews were so smug. They thought they had the best of everything—God's favor, pure blood, the temple. No matter how thirsty he was, this Jew would never drink from a Samaritan jug. His loss.

But as the woman pulled her bucket up from the well, the Jew spoke to her. He asked for a drink. Surprised, she muttered something about Jews and Samaritans not getting along.

Then the man said, "If you knew the gift of God and who it is that asks you for a drink, you would have asked him and he would have given you living water."

Right. There's that smugness again. He had no bucket; the well was deep. What does he think he is doing, offering her water? And living

25

water, no less. He meant running water, of course—much better than this well—but there wasn't a running stream for miles. Who did he think he was?

But he went on speaking in his strange way: "Everyone who drinks this water will be thirsty again, but whoever drinks the water I give him will never thirst. Indeed, the water I give him will become in him a spring of water welling up to eternal life."

That sounds good, the woman thought. "It's a real pain coming out here each day. Sign me up."

"Go call your husband and come back," the man said.

Oops. "Uh," she said, "I have no husband."

"You are quite right when you say you have no husband," he said. "The fact is, you have had five husbands, and the man you now have is not your husband. What you have said is quite true."

He knew! She had never seen him before, but he knew the details of her personal life. All five husbands! Why, even she lost count sometimes. But he knew! And still he was talking with her. A true Jew would steer clear of Samaria, would avoid talking with a strange woman, and would throw stones at one who couldn't keep a husband. This man was different. Perhaps he's a prophet, another Elisha, come to put Samaria back together, come to put her back together. And there he sat with that smug Jewish smile on his face, as if he were conjuring up the names of each of her husbands, the wedding dates, and just what unfaithfulness had caused each of her marriages to fail. She had never met a prophet before. What would he demand of her? How could she ever set things right?

But enough about me, she thought. *Let's talk theology. It's not often that you have a prophet in your parlor. Time to get your questions answered.*

"Sir," she said, "I perceive that you are a prophet. Our fathers worshiped on this mountain"—she pointed to the holy mount of Gerizim where, a thousand years earlier, Joshua had gathered the Israelites and had the priests declare God's blessing—"but you Jews claim that the place where we must worship is in Jerusalem."

Let's see what he does with this one, she thought. *Will he bend at all? Will he let the Samaritans be Samaritans? Will he honor our traditions? Or is he just another Jewish do-gooder trying to reunite the divided kingdom on Jewish terms?*

But Jesus set his own terms: "Believe me, woman, a time is coming when you will worship the Father neither on this mountain nor in

26

Jerusalem. You Samaritans worship what you do not know; we worship what we do know, for salvation is from the Jews. Yet a time is coming and has now come, when the true worshipers will worship the Father in spirit and truth, for they are the kind of worshipers the Father seeks. God is spirit, and his worshipers must worship in spirit and in truth."

It got a bit heavy for her, all this talk of spirit and truth. There was something there, something important. The stranger said the time "is coming and has come." *If he's right, perhaps Messiah will be here soon. Messiah will explain everything, will clear up the whole misunderstanding between Jews and Samaritans, will set things right.*

Jesus said, "I who speak to you am he."

People misunderstand Jesus' statements in John 4. Generally, they interpret it to mean: It doesn't matter where you worship because God is spirit; worship God in your spirit. Sounds good, but it is not entirely what Jesus is saying here.

"God is spirit." What does this mean? Most people take it to mean that God has no body. Spirit is the opposite of flesh, they figure. Thus they think Jesus is saying that God is not physical.

But they forget who was talking. Jesus. And who was Jesus? God-in-flesh. God has a body, the body of Jesus. God is physical—that's what Jesus' incarnation is all about. John fought valiantly in his writings, as did other leaders of the early church, against the notion that Jesus just "appeared" to be human, that his body was just an apparition. John goes into great detail in his Gospel to show Jesus touching people—drinking water, spitting on the ground, getting physically tired, bleeding, dying, eating breakfast. It is John who tells us about Thomas touching the wounds of Jesus after the Resurrection. It is John who prefaces his first letter with: "That which was from the beginning, which we have heard, which we have seen with our eyes, which we have looked at and our hands have touched—this we proclaim concerning the Word of life" (1 John 1:1).

Yet it is John who faithfully records Jesus' statement that "God is spirit." What does he mean?

We make our mistake by assuming that spirit is the opposite of body. Reading through the New Testament, we find "spirit" often set opposite to "flesh." Paul particularly wrote about living in the spirit and denying the flesh. On first glance, it appears that he was disparaging all that is physical. But that can't be. It would fly in the face of Hebrew tradition and thought. It would contradict Paul's own affirmation of

27

created things. But primarily it would nullify the Incarnation. If it is evil to be physical, what was Jesus doing with a body? If bodies are evil, why did God create them to begin with?

There is another small logical problem with the spirit/body anti-thesis. We are physical. There is no way we can't be. That is how God made us. For Scripture to ask us to be unphysical—well, that would be impossible. Sure, we can cultivate the life of the spirit, concentrate on spiritual things. We can deny the pleasures of the body. But we can't be any less physical than we are.

No, Paul meant something different by "flesh." (Here's another example of a word evolving in meaning. The New Testament takes the word *sarx,* "flesh," and attaches a whole new meaning to it.) When the New Testament urges us to be "spiritual," it is asking us to submit our bodies to the Spirit's control—body-and-spirit together. When it talks about "flesh," it is talking about denying the Spirit's involvement with our bodies, feeding our own bodily drives—body-without-spirit. In either case, we have bodies. The question is, Who's in control?

It might help to consider an alternate meaning of *spirit,* not only in English (from Latin), but in Greek and Hebrew as well—"breath." A body that breathes is a healthy body. A body that doesn't breathe is dead. That was what Paul said about spirit and flesh. When our bodies breathe God's Spirit, we are living as we were meant to. When the Spirit is not there, we're dead—and even though some bodily functions may continue, there is only a gradual process of decay ahead of us.

So when Jesus said, "God is spirit," he was not saying, "God is non-physical." That would be to deny his own identity. He was saying that God is breath, that God is in fact the breath of life, that he blows through temples and mountains and people and enlivens them.

In Genesis we read that God scooped up a handful of earth (*adamah,* in the Hebrew) and formed a man (Adam). He "breathed into his nostrils the breath of life, and the man became a living being" (Gen. 2:7). Elsewhere, Scripture reminds us that, apart from the breath of God, we are but handfuls of dirt. "He knows what we are made of," Psalm 103 says. "He remembers that we are dust." But God's breath, his Spirit, gives us life.

Why did Jesus say all this to the woman—about God being spirit? Because she was dying. When he first saw her coming to the well with the jug on her shoulder, he could see her life was as dusty as the ground

28

she walked on. She came to slake her thirst, but the well's water wouldn't last. She needed living water.

She was flesh, in the fullest sense of the New Testament. Her need for love and protection had driven her from one man to another. Perhaps her very sense of commitment was decaying, since she wasn't married to the man she was living with at the time. She had no breath blowing through her. She was all dust, no wind.

But she was dying in another way, too. In her formal worship. She at least paid lip-service to the Samaritan tradition of worship. We don't know whether she really worshiped on Mt. Gerizim, but she was ready to defend the tradition.

Jesus saw two problems with the worship at Gerizim, and he masterfully explained them. The first problem is one it shares with temple worship. It will not last. "A time is coming," Jesus said, "when you will worship the Father neither on this mountain nor in Jerusalem." Both are temporary.

Notice that, in this verse, Jesus did not say that worshiping in either place was bad. He was not saying it is wrong to worship in a formal setting, to follow traditions, to use liturgies. The problem with temple worship was the same as with the whole Jewish law—it was not complete. Jesus himself was the completion of the Law. He announced it in an early address: "Do not think that I have come to abolish the Law or the Prophets; I have not come to abolish them but to fulfill them" (Matt. 5:17). Later Paul explained that the law was a "schoolmaster"—the word (*paidagogos*) really refers to the servant who would lead a child safely to school—to bring us to Christ (Gal. 3:24).

There are times when Paul referred to the law in the same terms he used for flesh, so we need to see it in the same way. The law was given by the Spirit of God ("All Scripture is God-breathed"—2 Tim. 3:16) and, as the Spirit breathes through it, the law is wonderful. But the spirit of the law is supposed to lead a person to Christ. To stubbornly hold to the letter of the law while denying the spirit of it is "flesh." "The letter kills, but the Spirit gives life," Paul wrote (2 Cor. 3:6). The law is good, as long as the Spirit blows through it to lead one to Christ. But apart from the Spirit, it is deadly, and dying itself.

That lies behind Jesus' statements about the worship at the temple and on Gerizim. Perhaps he was looking ahead to the destruction of the temple in A.D. 70. The forms were fine for a time, but temporary. And once the keepers of the forms rejected the spirit of the forms, the forms became obsolete. Thus this woman's worship was decaying.

There was a second problem with the worship on Mt. Gerizim. It was not true. That is, it was not based on the true revelation of God. "You Samaritans worship what you do not know. We worship what we do know, for salvation is from the Jews."

That calls to mind Paul's sojourn in Athens, where he came across a shrine "To the Unknown God." They had idols for every god they could think of, but this altar was dedicated to the one whose power they acknowledged, but whose name they did not know. Paul told them, "What you worship as something unknown I am going to proclaim to you." He went on to tell them of the Creator, the Father, who raised Jesus from the dead (Acts 17).

Even today, many worship an unknown god. He's there, somewhere, when they need help, but they don't really want to know much about him. Many religions of the world shroud their gods in mystery, preserving their unknowableness. Certainly we do not know everything about our God; there is plenty of mystery to ponder. But God has also revealed himself to us.

And this is where temple worship and the worship on Gerizim parted company. Both were obsolete apart from the Spirit. But the Jews' tradition at least had the possibility of leading them on to Christ. That tradition was based on the utterances of God, and if people paid attention, they would find the complete truth in Jesus. The Samaritans, on the other hand, had assimilated a mix of traditions. They worshiped an unknown God.

"Salvation is from the Jews" sounds like a very chauvinistic thing to say, especially to a Samaritan. Jesus was not just being nationalistic, however; he was being very personal. He was a Jew, and apart from tours like this through Samaria, he spent virtually all his life in Judea and Galilee. He grew up in the Jewish law, taught as a Jewish rabbi. Most important, he was the fulfillment of the Jewish law. And he was salvation.

It may have been difficult for the woman to hear this. She had probably been brought up to believe that worshiping on Gerizim was just as good as worshiping in Jerusalem. She probably hoped he would agree.

Yes and no, he says. If the Spirit of God is absent, you're right: there is no difference. Both traditions are dead. But the Jewish faith, not the Samaritan tradition, can lead to the truth—the truth of Jesus.

Jesus then sums up his critique with two words, spirit and truth. This is how "true worshipers" will worship the Father.

First he announced the timing: "the time is coming, and has now come." Earlier he had announced the coming obsolescence of worship at the temple and on Mt. Gerizim. But he sets this declaration in the present. What's the difference? What marks the present time? How does he know "the time has now come"?

His own presence. He is what the world has been waiting for. He is the perfect embodiment of the Spirit. He is the Truth. He enables people to worship God truly.

So what does it mean to worship in spirit and truth?

Worship in the spirit does not mean nonphysical worship. It does mean that we mustn't let the physical forms of worship dominate to the point of shutting out the spirit. That would be the way of the flesh. Worship in the spirit lets the Spirit of God blow through our bodies, through the physical forms, to activate our minds (reminding us why we are worshiping and whom we are worshiping), our emotions (helping us feel honestly the joy and challenge of worshiping God), and our bodies (renewing our energies to worship in ways that please him).

The Spirit makes himself known in many ways. He is a Spirit of life, as we have already seen. He is a Spirit of power. His work explodes beyond the boundaries of formal worship and affects our daily lives. He is a Spirit of truth, leading us to greater understanding of God's revelation. He is, above all, the Spirit of Christ, who is the fullest expression of God's revelation.

When Jesus talked about truth, he was talking about himself. "I am the way, the truth, and the life," he said (John 14:6, KJV). Elsewhere, "You shall know the truth and the truth shall make you free" (John 8:32, NKJV). He was saying there, "You will know the truth about me, you will know the truth of me, you will truly know me." (When dealing with Jesus, the epitome of truth, it is hard to keep knowledge on a merely mental level. Truth demands our involvement.)

So when Jesus said that worshipers must worship in spirit and *truth*, we must remember that all the revealed truth of God in the Scriptures leads to him, the embodiment of that truth. He was saying that *he* is the way to worship the Father. Worshipers must come through him. "No one comes to the Father except through me" (John 14:6).

So we need to worship "in Christ," and in the truth of Christ. What does this mean? It means first of all that *we* need to be in Christ. We should know him personally, being personally regenerated by the Spirit, in order to truly worship him.

31

It also means that the declaration of truth about Jesus has an important place in our worship. We have seen this again and again in the New Testament examples, as worshipers have declared, "You are the Son of God," or words to that effect. Even in John 4, with the woman at the well, the passage ends with Jesus' declaration of his own messiahship. (And then the woman hurried to declare Jesus' identity to the town.)

It also means that our worship should be based on the revealed truth of God, the Bible. John saw an essential unity between Jesus and the Scriptures. The Scriptures testify of Jesus. In fact, Jesus is called the Word, as well as the Truth. Worshiping in Truth, in Christ, means letting the Spirit use the Scriptures to testify to Christ.

Let's fast-forward fifty years or so, from that Samaritan well to the church at Ephesus. John is writing this Gospel. The Spirit is bringing to his mind the words and actions of Jesus, and he is writing them down, organizing them, explaining them. He is teaching a new generation of Christians who Jesus was and what he meant.

The church of John's time faced two major foes: the legalists and the mystics. Yes, those Judaizers who followed Paul around were still plaguing the church. In fact, after the fall of Jerusalem in A.D. 70, a number of zealous Jews saw Christianity as the only hope for a revival of Judaism. They latched onto the church but brought with them their old ideas of the law being necessary for salvation.

Paul had fought vigorously against these ideas. "The law was dead," he insisted. "You believers have been enlivened by God's Spirit. Why do you want to crawl back into the grave?" This was still an issue when John was writing.

But John also has to contend with an assortment of mystical ideas about Jesus. The Gnostics invented all sorts of avenues to get to God. Angels and demigods could help you attain that secret knowledge that would set you apart from ordinary humans. The Christ-spirit was the supreme emanation from a Spirit-God—this spirit, some said, inhabited the man Jesus at his baptism and left before his death. You can find fullness, oneness with the Christ-spirit, by escaping from the control of your physical body.

False teachings were creeping into John's church. John had to distinguish between true and false. He had to throw out the heretics and nurture the true believers. You find that "we-they" attitude throughout his first epistle. It was essential to preserve the identity, the purity, the faithfulness of the church.

So as he writes about the woman at the well, John sees two things: a dead formalism and a mystical Samaritan faith not rooted in Scripture. He remembers Jesus' words and he marvels at how they apply to his world. "True worshipers . . . ," the apostle pens, and thinks of all the false worshipers threatening his beloved church; ". . . worship the Father in spirit . . . ," not in the dead legalism of the Judaizers, but in the vibrant life of God's Spirit; ". . . and in truth," not the half-baked fantasies of the Gnostics, but the true identity of Jesus, the Christ.

We still have to fight those heresies today. The legalists embrace the old forms and squeeze the life right out of them. The mystics rush at new ideas and run right past the Scriptures.

FIVE
THE CASE OF THE MISSING VERB
(ACTS 17 AND THE PASTORAL EPISTLES)

If you had a friend who was enamored with New Age teaching, and you were trying to explain the distinctions of Christianity, chances are you wouldn't talk about how Christ's Spirit helps us "achieve enlightenment."

You could, because the Spirit does. The Bible is rich with images of light. We are children of light. The Spirit shines in our hearts. The light shines in the darkness. And so on.

But if you talked about "enlightenment," this New Age devotee would probably lump Christianity in with Buddhism, Hinduism, and whatever Egyptian god he or she happened to be channeling at the moment. Like it or not, these religions have "claimed" that term. We can try to claim it back, but only with a lot of explanation and the possibility of serious misunderstanding.

It is easier to use another word.

That is what happened with Greek words for worship. If you walked up to someone in first-century Athens and asked, "What god do you worship?"—using the biblical word *proskuneo*, which we've been tracking so far—he might look at you funny. Or he would say, "Oh, you must be Jewish."

You see, the word Greeks used for the worship of their gods was *sebomai*. It had the physical sense of shrinking back in awe, but it had come to mean both an attitude of reverence and acts of devotion. That

35

sounds a lot like what we have been learning about biblical worship, but for some reason, the Jews didn't like *sebomai.*

When the seventy scholars translated the Hebrew Scriptures into Greek beginning about 250 B.C., they consistently neglected *sebomai.* When the Hebrew text had a word for worship, they regularly used *proskuneo* instead—which most Greeks would have considered a very ordinary word for bowing down, without any special religious meaning. In the few cases where the Jewish translators used *sebomai,* it was usually in some foreign or negative context.

For instance, Jonah explained to the foreign sailors, "I am a Hebrew and I worship [*sebomai*] Yahweh" (Jon. 1:9). The Septuagint translators were right. The sailors would *sebomai* their own gods. Jonah was speaking in terms they would understand. If they were his fellow Jews, he probably would have said (that is, it would have been translated), "I *proskuneo* Yahweh."

After the Lord pointed out Job's righteousness, the devil shot back, "Does Job fear [*sebomai*] God for nothing?" The devil was implying that Job was just paying his dues. All his religious devotion was merely an insurance premium to pay for God's protection. This is hardly a complimentary view of worship.

And through Isaiah, the Lord said:

> These people come near to me with their mouth
>   and honor me with their lips,
>   but their hearts are far from me.
> They worship [*sebomai*] me in vain;
>   their teachings are only the rules and teachings of men.
> (Isa. 29:13; Septuagint)

Jesus quoted this same passage in criticizing the Pharisees (Matt. 15:8-9). This is obviously another uncomplimentary view. Worship of the *sebomai* kind is often empty, vain, pointless, because it is insincere.

From these few biblical uses of the Greek word *sebomai,* we begin to compile a definition. From a Jewish point of view (at least among the translators of the Septuagint), *sebomai* is (1) the way foreigners worship their false gods; (2) a kind of payment for divine favor; (3) insincere rituals or prayers based on human teachings. These three senses go together, as indicated by Jesus' criticism of the hypocritical Pharisees: "And when you pray, do not keep on babbling like pagans, for they think they will be heard because of their many words" (Matt. 6:7).

Of course, the word had no such negative connotation in the Greek world. Your average Athenian would say *sebomai* was a good thing to do. It was not just a feeling, not just awe or fear. It involved action—showing reverence to the gods through prayers or acts of sacrifice. In fact, the Greeks coined a new word, *eusebia,* to indicate a whole new virtue. Literally, you might call it "goodworship." (*Eu* is Greek for "good" or "proper"; *sebia* comes from *sebomai.*) The *eusebes* person was devout, properly religious. Out of respect for the gods, he lived well, cared for his family, observed the proper rituals, had a positive mental outlook, was an upstanding member of the community—you get the idea.

In the five centuries before Jesus, there were two streams of religious thinking in the Greek world. These two words, *sebomai* and *eusebia,* seem to characterize them. First, there was the traditional worship of the gods, such as Zeus, Apollo, and Athena. Different regions had local deities (such as Artemis of the Ephesians mentioned in Acts 17). These gods had their altars, temples, priests, and rituals. Choose one or more and worship (*sebomai*) in the proper way.

But then the philosophers saw how silly all this was. They began talking in terms of "life force" and "reason" and "the order of the universe." It was still OK to *sebomai,* but some people got fanatical about it. The idea of "goodworship" implied that there was "bad-worship." The philosophers probably would have said that some worshipers went overboard. The ideal religious life was now *eusebia,* godliness.

You remember that *sebomai* originally meant shrinking back in awe or fear. Now, with *eusebia,* it became a stepping back to fully appreciate. If you watch a horror movie and see an ogre come at you with a scythe, you jump back. That is *sebomai.* But when your friend shows up with a fancy new car, what do you do? You step back, take it all in . . . "very nice!" That's *eusebia.*

By contrast, *proskuneo* is a kneeling in front of. It is the posture of a servant. Is this another reason why the Jewish translators chose this word instead of the more popular Greek terms? Maybe. Consider:

The *sebomai* person says, "God, you scare me to death. Therefore, I will do what I need to do just so you'll be nice to me instead of mean."

The *eusebia* person says, "Yes, God, or Life-force, or whatever your name is, you've arranged things very nicely. And I understand that if I do things the proper way, good things will result. So, with all my dignity intact, I will try to live wisely in the world you've set up." The *proskuneo* person says, "God, you are great, far greater than I am. But I don't shrink back, I don't run away. I offer myself before you as a servant, trusting in your mercy."

When we take all this into account, it is not surprising that we seldom find the word *sebomai* in the Gospels. We really don't encounter it much until we're well into the Book of Acts—at the point where Christianity invades the Greek world. Suddenly the Christians take up a dialogue with people whose whole idea of worship has been *sebomai* or *eusebia*. How do they explain Christian worship?

When Paul visited Athens, he hit the hotbed of Greek philosophy. Centuries earlier, Socrates, Plato, and Aristotle had walked those streets, pondering the mysteries of existence and ethics. Now the Epicureans and Stoics staged their debates, arguing the nature of the human soul.

The philosophers didn't deny religion. Perhaps they had learned from Socrates' sad end that it didn't pay to debunk the popular mythologies. But they went beyond religion. They worshiped the gods with appropriate rituals, then developed their philosophical systems, which had little room for deity.

So Athens had both—*sebomai* and *eusebia,* worship rituals and polite piety. It was a city full of idols and idle thinkers—a dangerous combination.

As usual, Paul began at the synagogue. Most of the major cities of the Roman Empire had pockets of Jewish civilization. The Jewish community of Athens would have had a synagogue, and that was where Paul went to present the gospel. Jews were generally eager to hear traveling rabbis, especially one with credentials as good as Paul's. So the apostle found a ready audience.

The Bible says Paul "reasoned [the Greek word is 'dialogued'] in the synagogue with the Jews and God-fearing Greeks" (Acts 17:17). Time out. The word for "God-fearing Greeks" is *sebomenois,* a form of *sebomai.* This is a specialized New Testament use of the word. Apparently, Judaism became rather popular in the Roman world. Gentiles were attracted by its monotheism and by its morality. Many Greeks longed for a sense of order that their pantheon of gods and goddesses could not provide. Yahweh, however, made sense to them, so they attached themselves to local synagogues. They did not all become full-fledged converts (some thought circumcision was too serious a commitment), but they attended services and tried to follow the teachings of Moses. These were known as "God-worshipers," *sebomenoi*—sometimes you'll see this translated "God-fearers" (Acts 13:43, 50; 16:14; 17:4; 18:7).

From what we know of *sebomai*, it seems to fit. These Gentiles were standing back and appreciating the beauty of Judaism, but they weren't quite kneeling in servanthood-worship (*proskuneo*) before the Lord.

Still, the gospel found hungry hearts among both Jews and Gentile God-worshipers. Though there was often opposition, the synagogues generally provided the first converts for the local churches.

In Athens, Paul began to debate with Epicurean and Stoic philosophers, who invited him (or possibly subpoenaed him) to appear before the local philosophers' council, the esteemed Areopagus. There he began by saying, "Men of Athens, I see that in every way you are very religious."

Paul chose his words carefully, and he used a masterpiece here. The word for "very religious" comes from *deisidaimonia—Desdemona*, if you will. Hidden within is the word *daimon*, which comes into English as *demon*. It actually referred to any supernatural power, good or bad. The Athenians had just accused Paul of being a proclaimer "of strange gods" (*daimonia*). They weren't sure yet whether his *daimons* were good or bad. So Paul turned the tables by saying, "You seem very concerned about *daimonia*." His meaning could be taken two ways. He could be saying, in a nice way, "You're very religious." Or he could be saying (as the King James Version puts it), "You are too superstitious." It is quite possible that Paul intended this double meaning, keeping them on the edge of their seats, waiting to hear his conclusions. Would he affirm their religious sentiments or trash them? He did a little of both.

"I was looking at your objects of worship." The word is *sebasmata* (related to *sebomai*), things that are worshiped.

"And I found an altar with this inscription: To An Unknown God." The Arlington National Cemetery has a Tomb of the Unknown Soldier, honoring all those who died in battle but whose bodies were not recovered or identified. The officials who planned this monument wanted to be sure not to deprive any war hero of his proper honor. The Athenian altar was similar. The city was full of idols, but some deity might have been missed. These Greeks wanted to be sure not to offend any god by depriving him of a worship site.

"The one you worship [*eusebia*] unknowingly, he's the one I declare to you." As we've seen, there is something polite about *eusebia*. It is not a flounce-around-and-shout-at-the-top-of-your-lungs kind of worship. It is a matter of respect, doing your duty for the gods and your fellowman. A lot of Americans worship this way. And, in fact, it was the Athenians' politeness that made them put up this altar. We wouldn't want to offend any god, now would we?

But it's this same bridge-club, tea-party mentality that made *eusebia* an inappropriate concept for Christian worship. Worshiping the Almighty God of all is not a matter of sending engraved thank-you notes—it involves bowing in humble service before him.

Someone might argue that the Athenians were really acting out of fear. They were terrified that some unworshiped god might be offended and send some disaster on their city. This may well be, and it adds a fascinating angle to this idea of politeness.

In some social circles today, politeness is driven by fear. People do the social graces for each other because they are afraid they may be blacklisted, scorned, or slandered if they don't. In their purest form, "manners" are merely expressions of love and respect. I hold a door open for my date because I care for her and want to show this. But what happens when I hold the door open because I'm afraid she'll hate me if I don't? My action is suddenly not loving but grudging. I begin to do this act of respect out of selfish desire. Something is seriously wrong with this relationship.

That was the problem with the Athenians' *eusebia*. They did their devotions out of fear, not love. They scurried to keep all the gods (or *daimons*) happy, so they could live their lives in peace. What they saw as a reasonable religion was really driven by deep superstition.

Paul went on to introduce God to the Athenians in a flurry of lofty language. We'll hit his main points.

1. God the Creator is Lord of heaven and earth—not just one pocket of dominion. He is Lord of all. This would have struck sympathetic chords with some of the Greek philosophers. Since Socrates, there had been a move toward monotheism. Most Greeks were still avid polytheists, but a number of philosophers were talking about a "henotheism"—one ruling God over all the other gods.

2. God does not live in man-made temples. Temples dotted the Roman Empire, devoted to scores of deities. Cities built temples so

that their gods would come and live there. It was assumed that Paul's God, the God of the Jews, lived in the Jerusalem temple. This statement by Paul might have surprised many.

3. God is "not served by human hands, as if he needed anything, because he himself gives all men life and breath and everything else." The word for "served" here is *therapeuo*. You can see the word *therapeutic* in it. It is as if we try to put God in a hospital bed and play nurse. This doesn't work, Paul said. The Athenians, as we have seen, were just trying to keep the gods happy. Extending the image, it was as if they were a lone nurse on a busy hospital floor, with Zeus and Apollo and Aphrodite and other gods as patients in the hospital rooms. The Athenians went running from room to room (from temple to temple), to make sure nothing went wrong. Paul said it was wrong to make God our patient. He is the one who heals us.

4. People do seek God. Paul's comments in Acts 17:26-27 were echoed later in his first chapter to the Romans. God's creation and his control of history leave a powerful witness. Those who are paying attention will seek to know the Lord who made them. Here Paul spoke of people "reaching out" and finding the Lord. It was a picture of hands groping and grabbing onto something real. Jesus used the same Greek word (*pselaphao*) after his resurrection when he told the disciples, "Touch me" (Luke 24:39), to make sure he had really risen. And John may have been remembering that scene as he opened his first epistle: "That which. . . our hands have touched [*pselaphao*]. . . this we proclaim" (1 John 1:1).

People want to grab onto something real, tangible. Many of the Greeks fashioned idols of silver or gold, and housed them in temples. This was their way of reaching out and touching their gods.

5. God is not far from us. We are, in fact, his children. Paul added to the picture: People are reaching out, but they are reaching too far. God is right there next to them. It is the everyday image of the person who looks all over the house for his glasses when they are on top of his head. Similarly, the Greeks scampered to honor all their idols, when they themselves were the children of the Creator God. The word for children here is not the warm, personal word we find elsewhere in the New Testament. It has little to do with a personal relationship. It is purely physical—*genos,* offspring, stock. Paul was not saying, "Rejoice! You are in God's family!" He was saying, "All of us human beings are made in God's image, we come from his stock, so why are we bowing before hunks of metal?"

6. The proper way to worship God is through the risen Jesus. It only makes sense. God is not a mineral; he is a person like us (beyond us, but like us) and he deals with us in personal ways—specifically through the person of Jesus.

And up to this point, the philosophers, at least the progressive ones, might have been smiling. They probably thought of themselves as miles ahead of the common people. They already had this feeling that the silver and gold idols were just for show, that the real divine force floated in and around them. So they probably liked Paul's comments about being "God's offspring." After all, some Greek philosopher-poets had already been saying that.

But the idea that one man was appointed by God and raised from the dead was a scandal. It didn't fit into their belief system. They may have been very religious, or superstitious, but their *daimons* didn't have that kind of power. Their idea of God was too small to pack in a physical resurrection.

The text gives the impression that Paul was hooted down by dissenting members of the council. While some wanted to hear more, the majority apparently wanted him thrown out.

But Paul wasn't finished with *eusebia*. Late in his ministry, he began to reclaim the word, to give it a Christian use. We see it often (translated "godliness") in 1 and 2 Timothy and in Titus, probably the last letters he wrote.

Let's review the history of this word. It was derived from *sebomai*, the kind of fearful worship pagans do. With a literal meaning of "goodworship," it came to mean responsible piety—being a good person, doing one's duty, not getting too crazy. It became a virtue in Greek society.

Now, this is not a bad idea. God's people should be good and responsible. We can only guess at why the word seldom appears in Jewish or early Christian writings. Probably the idea of being good wasn't good enough. In the Jewish Scriptures, being an upstanding member of the community wasn't nearly as important as being an obedient servant of God. And Christianity wasn't a matter of doing one's duty as much as responding to God's grace and mercy. The early Christians didn't care a whole lot about maintaining dignity as good citizens—they were radical disciples, sacrificing their dignity, if need be, for the cause of Christ.

But the word *eusebia* also carried a nice little idea that Paul apparently liked. *Eusebia* was worship that you lived out in your everyday life. It wasn't just a thought or a feeling—it was a devotion expressed in how you talked, in how you cared for your family, in how you treated your neighbor. If Paul could just shake the word free from its "politeness," from its "I'm doing my bit for God so that he'll be nice to me"—he could use *eusebia* to express good Christian sentiments. Apparently by the mid-sixties, he decided to try.

Two things were happening at the time. First, Paul was going to die soon, and he knew it. The church needed good leadership and good organization to lead into future generations. The honeymoon was over, in a way. Christians needed to pay more attention to how they treated each other. They needed to be responsible "citizens" of the church. Thus, *eusebia* would be an important virtue.

Second, the church needed good PR. For the first few decades, Christianity was under the umbrella of Judaism. Jews enjoyed certain protections as a legal religion within the Roman Empire, and these were extended to Christians. But by the early sixties, officials were beginning to realize that Christians were different from Jews. Rumors were flying about Christianity's strange rituals, eating the "body" and "blood" of the "Son" and showing love for the "brothers and sisters." It certainly sounded like cannibalism, child-sacrifice, and incest. In A.D. 64, Nero stirred up these rumors and blamed the Christians for setting a disastrous fire in Rome. The heat was on, so to speak. Persecution began.

Paul was writing to Timothy and Titus between 63 and 67—in the midst of these events. It was crucial for Christians to debunk the rumors by living respectable lives in society. If they just lived out their devotion to Christ, they would be good citizens. They would demonstrate the self-control, the kindness, and the sobriety that Roman society prized. And so, *eusebia* became a Christian virtue.

This "good citizenship" is seen first in 1 Timothy 2:2. Paul told the young pastor to lead his congregation in prayers "for kings and all those in authority, that we may live peaceful and quiet lives in all godliness [*eusebia*] and holiness [the Greek word has more to do with sobriety or reverence]." As if Timothy might be surprised that Paul was suddenly promoting this secular virtue, the apostle added, "This is good, and pleases God our Savior."

In 1 Timothy 5:4, Paul challenged the children and grandchildren of needy widows to "put their religion into practice" [*eusebeo*] by supporting their own family. Any book of Roman etiquette would agree:

family duties were important in that society. But Paul added, "This is pleasing to God."

The apostle may be explaining the difference between the new *eusebia* and the old in 2 Timothy 3:5, describing people of "the last days": "having a form of godliness [*eusebia*] but denying its power." That was the problem with "polite" *eusebia*. It had some nice forms, but it lacked the power of God. Christian godliness would be more than politeness; it would be fueled by God's power and love.

The "mystery of godliness [*eusebia*]" is set forth in 1 Timothy 3:16. It is a hymn about Jesus. The Lord himself is the source of our good living. In his first verse to Titus, Paul wrote of "the knowledge of the truth that leads to godliness [*eusebia*]." Make no mistake. Our respectable lives are not just good citizenship, but the natural outgrowth of the truth of the gospel.

In 1 Timothy 6:5-6, Paul criticized those "who think that godliness [*eusebia*] was a means to financial gain." The old polite *eusebia* always had a sense of quid pro quo—I do this in order to get divine (or social) favor. That kind of thinking is out, Paul said. "But godliness with contentment is great gain." Living out your faith may win some friends for you, it may lose some, but it won't make you rich. On the contrary, Paul warned, "Everyone who wants to live a godly [*eusebos*] life in Christ Jesus will be persecuted" (2 Tim. 3:12). Twenty years earlier, a Roman might have written, "Anyone who tries to live according to *eusebia* [that is, a respectable life] should run for the Senate." But Paul was sitting in a Roman jail. His "*eusebia* in Christ Jesus" would hurt, but it would please God.

So what do these Greek words, *sebomai* and *eusebia*, teach us about worship? And what do we learn from Paul's dealings with them in Athens and in his pastoral letters?

From the Jewish and early Christian nonuse of *sebomai* and *eusebia*, we can surmise:

1. Biblical worship differs in some key respect from the "natural" worship offered by "Gentiles." Although there seems to be an inborn need to worship, which is expressed by many cultures in many different ways, biblical writers saw their worship of God as being a very distinct thing.

2. Biblical worship is less of a shrinking back in fear and more of a bowing in humility.

3. Biblical worship is not some sort of payment to God—either bribe or insurance—to get him to do something nice for us or to keep

him from being nasty. Pagan cultures seemed to see worship this way, but Scripture avoids this angle.

From Paul's speech to the Athenians, we learn:

4. God is not confined to temples. Presumably, we may worship him anywhere.

5. God does not need our worship. He wants it, but it is not as if we keep God alive by our ministry to him.

6. The proper way to worship God is through the risen Jesus.

From Paul's "reclaiming" of *eusebia* in his pastoral epistles, we learn:

7. Proper worship of God extends into our everyday lives, in how we treat other people and exercise self-control in our own lives.

8. The worship of Jesus, in fact, empowers us to live godly lives.

SIX
LIVING SACRIFICES
(ROMANS 12)

The Epistle to the Romans is foundational to Christian theology. As you might expect, it also provides a foundation for our theology of worship.

The first eight chapters lay out a logical explanation of the human need for salvation. Like a lawyer, Paul built his case: Jews and Gentiles alike are sinners, deserving death; God justifies people through faith, not works; Christ's obedient sacrifice has set us free from the law, free from the grip of sin; though we still struggle with sin, and long for eventual redemption, the Spirit strengthens us and reassures us that we are God's children.

But in chapter 9, Paul plunged into a gnarly issue: What about the Jews who have rejected Jesus? For three chapters, in deep, soul-searching language, the "apostle to the Gentiles" explored the status of his own people, the Jews. Why has God allowed the majority of his people to turn away, saving only a remnant? This is, in a sense, the question of the ages, the problem of evil, of sin, of unbelief. How could God let this happen?

His answer: I don't know. God does what he does because he wants to. That's all. No silver lining. No pot of gold at the end of the rainbow. No easy answers. It is a mystery wrapped up in the mind of God. Paul concluded, not with the air of Agatha Christie solving a case, but with a majestic benediction.

Oh, the depth of the riches of the wisdom
  and knowledge of God!
How unsearchable his judgments,
  and his paths beyond tracing out!
"Who has known the mind of the Lord?
  Or who has been his counselor?"
"Who has ever given to God,
  that God should repay him?"
For from him and through him and to him are all things.
To him be the glory forever! Amen.
  (Rom. 11:33-36)

God's wisdom is so far beyond ours, we can't always figure out why he does things. "His ways are above our ways."

Paul quoted two Old Testament passages. The first is from Isaiah 40: "Who has understood the mind of the LORD, or instructed him as his counselor?" There, God was comforting his captive people. No doubt they were questioning the fate that had befallen them as they languished in Babylon. But God promises deliverance and asserts his superiority over idols. He mocks those who create idols and then worship them. It just does not make sense to worship something inferior to yourself. Worship the one who created you. God may not have done things as you wished, but who are you to advise him? Do you know enough to tell him what to do?

The second quotation—"Who has ever given to God, that God should repay him?"—is from Job. Job had many reasons to wonder what God was doing. After his friends tried out all their arguments, the Lord himself spoke. As in Isaiah, he asserted his superiority over creation. "Who has a claim against me that I must pay?" he asked. "Everything under heaven belongs to me." God doesn't owe us anything.

With this background, Paul launched his summarizing statement: From him and through him and to him are all things.

From him: God created all that is. He is our source, our origin. We owe him our very existence.

Through him: God sustains all of life by his power. As the Greek poet wrote, "In him we live and move and have our being" (Acts 17:28). He is our strength, our breath. We owe him each moment of our lives.

To him: God ultimately receives all glory. He is the reason for all that is, the purpose of life. He created all things for his pleasure. We owe him our futures.

Thus God is the starting line, the finish line, and the race itself. He is the alpha and omega—and all the letters in between.

Because of his overarching supremacy, he has the right to do anything he wants. We have no right to second-guess.

Then Paul turned the corner into Romans 12. He was about to talk about Christians' responsibility to each other. At first glance, it seems disjointed. This Epistle had part 1, the theology lesson of chapters 1-8; part 2, the tough question about the Jews in 9-11; and now part 3, how the church works, 12-16. But chapter 12 is integrally connected with what goes before.

"Therefore, I urge you, brothers . . . ," Paul began. Some pundit scholar has said, when you see a "therefore," you need to ask, "What's it there for?" It means, "On the basis of what I've just said, here's some more good stuff." In this case, Paul was saying, "Because all things are from God and through God and to God, here is what you need to do."

What's more, he *urged* his readers to do this. I love the earnestness of the King James: "I beseech you." And he called them brothers. The deep feeling of the previous chapters is continued here. Paul had been mourning for his "brethren, my kinsmen according to the flesh" (9:3, KJV), that is, the Jews. Then he turned to his spiritual brothers, many of whom were believing Jews, and he urged them to respond properly to this great God.

Earlier, he had borrowed Isaiah's striking picture of God inviting his people into fellowship, but being ignored. "All day long I have held out my hands to a disobedient and obstinate people" (Rom. 10:21; Isa. 65:2). That is hardly the way to respond to the Creator, the Sustainer, the Purpose of Life. Here, Paul urged the faithful to respond rightly.

Paul also invoked God's mercy. This is a theme we have seen throughout Romans. Despite the sins of human beings, God has mercifully offered reconciliation and righteousness through Jesus. The Greek word used for mercy here means "compassion," looking on a helpless person with pity. The last time Paul used this word was in chapter 9, with God's stark statement from Exodus (regarding Pharaoh): "I will have mercy on whom I have mercy, and I will have compassion on whom I have compassion" (v. 15). The clear message of Romans is that we are the helpless ones. We deserve death and can do nothing to save ourselves. If God chooses to save us, he will. We are, very literally, at his mercy.

And God has had mercy on us. Paul was writing to believers, those who have said yes to God. So there are now two reasons for a positive response to the Lord (which Paul was about to describe). First, God is the supreme Creator-Sustainer-Purpose. Second, he has shown mercy to us.

Therefore—and here is finally the appropriate response—we must offer our bodies "as living sacrifices, holy and pleasing to the Lord."

Living sacrifices. The Romans would have considered that an oxymoron. You know, like "guest host" or "jumbo shrimp" or (in some churches) "short sermon." It is a contradiction in terms. A sacrifice dies—that's the whole point. You take the bull or the ram to the altar and kill it.

Some of the cults in the Roman Empire at the time may have even practiced human sacrifice. Devotion to those deities was so fanatical that adherents would give their lives as sacrifices. (Even today, young Muslims in Iran march to war, facing almost certain death, for the sake of Allah. These, in a way, are human sacrifices.) So the idea of offering your body as a sacrifice would not have been so strange—though it may have caused some consternation. But a living sacrifice?

Isaac was a living sacrifice. He had, no doubt, heard the stories from his aged parents of how they were promised a son. At first, they laughed—in fact, Isaac's name means "laughter"—but they trusted God's promise. Sure enough, Isaac was born.

Now, Scripture doesn't tell us much about the boy Isaac. But it doesn't take much to imagine that he might have been a bit cocky about his position as the child of promise. What could possibly happen to him?

But then his father, Abraham, packed up the donkey, and they set out for Mount Moriah. They had all the gear to make a burnt sacrifice, but there was something missing.

"Er, Dad?" he asked. "We have the torch and the wood, but aren't we forgetting something? What are we going to sacrifice? Where's the lamb?"

Abraham's reply was entirely too serious. "God will provide a lamb, my son." Did Isaac hear his father's voice crack?

They reached the mountain and built the altar, carefully piling the wood. And as Isaac looked around for the animal God would provide,

Abraham solemnly put his arms around his son and carried him to the altar. There he began to tie him down.

Isaac must have been stunned. "Wait, Dad, I'm your son. I'm the child God promised, remember? You can't kill me. God's going to make a great nation out of me—you told me that yourself. This can't be happening."

And the aged father raised the knife above his son's helpless body. A voice crackled like thunder: "Abraham!"

He stopped, the knife poised above his head, ready to plunge into Isaac's chest.

"Abraham! Do not hurt the boy." The voice came clearly now. Isaac breathed again. "Now I know that you fear God," the voice went on, "because you have not withheld from me your son, your only son."

The knife went clattering to the stones as Abraham hurried to untie his child. Isaac felt his father's warm embrace; he heard the old man's pounding heart. And then he faintly heard the bleat of a ram, caught in the thicket.

How would that have changed Isaac? If he was cocky before this, he could not have been afterward. His life belonged to God. God had given it in the first place, and God showed that he could take it at any time. Isaac was a living sacrifice.

The next we see of him, he is meditating in a field (Gen. 24:63). Perhaps his brush with death had made him more contemplative. Later we see him in a series of disputes over water rights—a significant economic matter in arid Palestine. He gives in, again and again, rather than fighting for his rights. Rights? What are rights? The Lord gives and the Lord takes away. If you take my well, God will provide another. Blessed be the name of the Lord. This is a "living sacrifice" mentality.

So Paul urged us to respond to this supreme God by putting ourselves on the altar. Note that this is not just some spiritual exercise—our *bodies* are to be presented for his service. And just as the sacrificial animals of Old Testament Israel were to be without spot or blemish, so our lives are to be "holy, acceptable to the Lord." This falls in line with the repeated messages in Isaiah, Amos, and elsewhere that the sacrifices of Israel stank—the incense was a stench in God's nostrils—because the people carried on in willful sin. Oppression of the poor, sexual immorality, greed, idolatry: these were sins of body and heart, nullifying the religious sacrifices they brought. The "living sacrifice" mentality means that we offer our lives in obedience to God.

The problem with living sacrifices is that they keep crawling off the altar. We sin. We indulge in oppression, immorality, greed, idolatry. We become unholy, unacceptable. But Paul had already established that our only hope of holiness is Jesus. The righteousness of the Beloved Son "in whom I am well-pleased" is put into our account, making us pleasing to God. When we sin, we can be forgiven. We can return to the altar, holy again.

Worship is the process of crawling back onto the altar. We present ourselves again as living sacrifices each time we return to worship the Lord.

Paul concluded verse 1 with a fascinating definition. This, he said, is your spiritual worship. The King James Version has it: "which is your reasonable service." It is not far off.

The word for "worship" (or "service") is not *proskuneo,* the falling-down-on-one's-face word we traced earlier. It is *latreia,* used specifically for religious observance, particularly the work of priests and Levites in the temple. It was work to light the candles, fill the bowls, perform the sacrifices, etc. And this word refers to the work of worship.

The word for "spiritual" (or "reasonable") is not related to the usual word for "spirit" (or "Holy Spirit"), *pneuma,* as you might expect. It is *logiken.* You can see the word *logical* in it, or the term *logos,* "word" or "reason." At one time in the Greek language, the word did mean "logical," and it is possible that it still carried that meaning in Paul's time. In that case, Paul would be saying, "It only makes sense—in light of God's supremacy and his mercy—it is only logical that you present your bodies as living sacrifices."

But the word changed meaning through time, influenced by Greek philosophy. The *logos* became the territory of the mind *as opposed to the body*—and therefore the idea of spirit got wrapped up in it. "Logical" (*logiken*) things were beyond the material realm, eternal, spiritual. The only other New Testament use of the word is in 1 Peter 2:2, where the apostle urged his readers to be like infants, craving "pure spiritual [*logiken*] milk," as opposed to the world's hate and hypocrisy. Peter went on to present a picture amazingly like that of Romans 12:1. "You also, like living stones, are being built into a spiritual [*pneumatikos*] house to be a holy priesthood, offering spiritual [*pneumatikos*] sacrifices acceptable to God through Jesus Christ" (1 Pet. 2:5). It is almost as if Peter were writing a commentary on Romans 12:1!

The word *logiken,* then, seems to raise the discussion to a higher level. It says, "Hey, we're not just talking about physical things here—we're talking eternal; we're talking spiritual." So Peter talks about Christian growth in terms of "spiritual" nutrition and then sets up this whole picture of the church as a new kind of temple, a new kind of priesthood, offering acceptable sacrifices.

Paul had just been discussing Israel in Romans 9-11. He called the Jews "my brothers according to the flesh." Later he affirmed that Christ himself was a Jew "according to the flesh." He acknowledged that God gave Israel lots of benefits: "the adoption . . . , the divine glory, the covenants, . . . the law, the temple worship [*latreia*], and the promises." But he added that not all who are Abraham's children "of the flesh" are truly children of God, that is, the "children of the promise."

Then in Romans 12:1, he said to the Christians, in effect, "You are my spiritual brothers. You are a new kind of Israel. You will offer sacrifices too, but *living* sacrifices. These will be holy, acceptable sacrifices. We are not talking about the physical 'of-the-flesh' temple worship [*latreia*] of the old days, which was prone to so many abuses. This is *spiritual* worship—the service of God kicked to a higher plane."

So what does all of this teach us about worship?

1. Worship is a basic, appropriate response to a God from whom and through whom and to whom are all things.

2. Worship "answers" unanswerable questions. We may not know God's purposes, but we can still praise him for them.

3. Christian worship flows not only from God's supremacy, but also from his mercy.

4. Christian worship is a new kind of temple-worship (*latreia*). Thus we can look to the Old Testament temple service for some models— even as we observe certain major differences.

5. The biggest difference is that we present not burnt sacrifices of bulls or goats, but living sacrifices of our bodies. We commit ourselves to live lives that are "holy, acceptable to God."

SEVEN
SNAPSHOTS
(ACTS 1-3)

It has been years since our family got out the slide projector and flashed our family history onto the living room wall. But when we did, it was great fun. At first we watched our cross-country trip. . . . There are Grandma and Grandpa in their beloved garden in Illinois. . . . There's that strange statue of Jesus in the Ozarks. . . . There's the Grand Canyon. And along with the pictures went the stories. . . . the steakhouse in Texas . . . the car overheating in Death Valley . . . meeting relatives by chance in Colorado.

Later we dabbled in Super 8 film. We took trips to Europe and the Holy Land. We saw ourselves growing up on the screen. The little nerdy kid with glasses became the big nerdy kid with glasses. My older brother's shirt in one scene would be my shirt in a picture a few years later. Little Kathy was always cute as a button. There was Ken as a teenager leading vacation Bible school ("Living Ken," they called him). And a few years later, there's "Dandy Randy" doing the same thing. Faces from the past float through these pictures. . . . "Whatever happened to . . . ?" Old girlfriends and boyfriends we would rather forget. Some we can't. Always, there were pictures . . . and stories.

The New Testament is the church's slideshow. Images from our past appear in Acts and the Epistles. We see the church in its infancy, growing up, learning to survive, learning to worship.

Amazingly, the New Testament doesn't tell us much about how to worship. We don't get seven-point outlines or preprinted church bulletins. But it does give us snapshots, glimpses of the church at worship. They aren't always flattering. But we can still learn from them.

My family learned early that we can't show our slides to everyone. People start yawning halfway through the first carousel. The exciting details of our family life are foreign to them. Maybe you have visited newlyweds who bring out the five photo albums of the wedding. "Here I am at the back of the church. And here I am near the back of the church, but more toward the middle. And here I . . ." They can flip through these albums every night—it's their wedding, a momentous occasion in their lives. But you're on the outside, and therefore a bit bored.

With the church, we're on the inside. It's our family. These are our stories. And what the church did back then has laid the groundwork for what we do today.

I know you're dying to crack open the church's photo album and see all these historical snapshots, but one more thing. There are people who look at historical photographs and analyze them psychologically. I saw this on a TV talk show, so I know it's true. They will see Churchill and Stalin and FDR shaking hands at Yalta and say, "Look at their eyes. You can see the Cold War coming."

They do that with family pictures, too. "Uncle Ed seems to be smiling, but he's giving Aunt Sally a scornful look." And, sure enough, they're divorced two years later. OK, I admit that's kind of crazy, but I can understand the principle as I look at pictures from my own past. I see tendencies that have stayed with me. Sure, I've grown; I've changed, but the seeds of what I am today were already planted and growing in that nerdy-looking ten-year-old with glasses.

And that is also true of the Christian church. The conflicts and joys and trials and strengths of the early church are essentially the same today. So we really can see ourselves in those Corinthians and Ephesians of old. The way they worshiped grew into the way we worship. That can give us a helpful perspective as we analyze our worship services.

We open the Book of Acts and read again of Jesus ascending into heaven. This is Luke's sequel—"Jesus, Part Two: The Saga Continues." He had finished Part One (the Gospel of Luke) with Jesus doing the divine equivalent of riding off into the sunset. Now, as in any good movie sequel, he begins where he left off.

"As we last left our Hero, he was giving his disciples last-minute instructions. . . . " Luke expanded slightly on Jesus' "You are witnesses" teaching from Luke 24:47-49. And he reiterated Jesus' command to stay in the city and wait for some special gift from the Father. Then Jesus ascended.

And then what?

There they are, in our first snapshot, Jesus' disciples standing on a mountainside, looking up into the air. What is the first order of business for this new church? Waiting.

It's never easy to wait. We wait in bank lines and doctors' offices, and it drives us crazy. The four-year-old counts the days until Christmas, sees the package under the tree, and waits. But at least the kid knows when Christmas is. "How many days till Christmas, Daddy?" And Daddy answers, "Two more days, Jenny, and then you can open your gift." But for the disciples, Daddy wasn't talking. "It is not for you to know the times or dates the Father has set," Jesus had told them in answer to their childlike question. They just waited. Maybe today. Maybe today.

Ten days they waited. And by waiting they were obeying what was probably a difficult command. Most of them were Galileans. Jerusalem was not home to them. It was full of threats. Immediately after Jesus' resurrection, they had met in secret for fear of reprisals by the authorities. Jesus' frequent postresurrection appearances must not have helped any. The authorities had figured that killing Jesus would stop him, but somehow even that had not worked. They must have dismissed the reports of the risen Jesus appearing here and there throughout their realm, but they probably assumed the disciples had launched a massive publicity drive to keep these rumors going.

When the disciples returned from the Mount of Olives after Jesus ascended, they were probably looking over their shoulders. They probably climbed the stairs to that same upper room where they had eaten the Last Supper and where Thomas had touched the risen Lord.

No, waiting is never easy, especially when you are afraid the government might nab you. Yet the disciples quietly obeyed their Lord.

What did they do while they waited? "They all joined together constantly in prayer," Luke wrote (Acts 1:14). This was probably in some side room of the temple complex. The group numbered 120 at the time, too many to cram into an upper room. The temple had numerous meeting rooms, and Luke indicated that the disciples "stayed continually at the temple, praising God" (Luke 24:53). This seems like very public behavior for wanted men. The authorities must have known they were at the temple—why didn't they arrest them? The authorities were probably still hoping that the Jesus movement would die out quietly. Though the disciples may have feared reprisals, we have no record of any active persecution of believers between the Crucifixion and Pentecost. An arrest at this point might have made matters worse. Both the Jewish leaders and the Roman officials seemed to have a keen sensitivity to public opinion. They consistently did their dirty work at night. Arresting the disciples at the temple in broad daylight would be bad for public relations. Still, we would expect the authorities to keep an eye on Jesus' followers—in case things started to get out of hand (which is exactly what happened in the next few chapters of Acts).

So Jesus' disciples were taking a certain risk when they met at the temple openly with other believers. Yet they must have felt it was very important to meet together in these days for prayer. But what did this "praying together" sound like? Did they all speak in unison? If so, what did they say? Was it some liturgical text from the synagogue or something from the Psalms? Was it perhaps the Lord's Prayer that they remembered from Jesus' teachings? We know from other texts (Luke 24:53; Acts 4:24-30) that praise was involved, as well as requests for God's strength. But did one person, maybe Peter, lead and the others say amen? Or did they take turns praying aloud, extemporaneously? Or did they all pray silently?

This was a new thing, this praying together. Prayer, as it appears throughout the Old Testament, and even in Jesus' ministry, was generally an individual thing. Abraham prayed. Moses prayed. Samuel prayed. Occasionally you will find a special occasion where some leader, a Joshua or Solomon, led the nation in prayer. And the Jewish synagogue certainly had its prayers, but these were generally liturgical formulations. The "prayer meeting" is not found until here in Acts. Even in Gethsemane, Jesus took his three select disciples to pray with him—but then he went off by himself, and they fell asleep anyway. Prayer had been individual communion with God, until this time. In Acts 1, the incipient church began to pray together, creating a new innovation in worship.

To convey this togetherness, Luke used the word *homothumadon*, which literally means "with the same passion." (Acts 1:14 reads literally, "They all persevered with the same passion in prayer. . . .")

This is one of Luke's favorite words. He used it eleven times in Acts—but never in his Gospel. It often describes the church's gatherings (Acts 2:1, 46; 4:24; 5:12; 15:25), but also refers to collective opposition to the church or the apostles (in Ephesus, the worshipers of Artemis seized Paul's companions and rushed "as one man" into the theater). The only other biblical use is by Paul, who prayed that the Romans would receive "a spirit of unity among yourselves as you follow Christ Jesus, so that with one heart [homothumadon] and mouth you may glorify the God and Father of our Lord Jesus Christ" (Rom. 15:5-6).

In other Greek writings, the word is often political, indicating a decision by consensus. It refers to situations in which people may differ on this point or that, but they felt strongly enough about the main idea that they would join together in some specific action. This is the sense twice in Acts, where representatives of the bickering kingdoms of Tyre and Sidon "joined together" to make peace with Herod (Acts 12:20) and where various groups of Jews "made a united attack on Paul" (Acts 18:12). The word homothumadon is used in both places.

Certainly we understand that the church was not free from disagreements. Even in Jesus' ministry, the disciples were elbowing each other for prominence in Christ's kingdom. And it was only six weeks earlier that they had scattered rather than face the threat of crucifixion with Jesus. Some of the early followers thought the women's report of resurrection was "nonsense" (Luke 24:11). Peter was still worried about what role John would get to play in the kingdom (John 21:21). It doesn't take too much imagination to think that there might have been some personality conflicts there. But, in obedience to their Lord, putting aside their differences, they wait together in Jerusalem and pray "with one accord."

One more item of business in Acts 1 is, quite literally, an item of business. They reorganized. Judas was gone; the believers decided to replace him. They held a business meeting, the nominating committee put forth two names, they drew lots, and Matthias was selected.

This is the first leaf of our photo album. We see the newborn church (perhaps the preborn church) waiting, obeying, praying (together), and organizing.

So what does all this have to do with worship?

So far in this book we have been looking at words. We have been asking, simply, "What does it mean to worship?" And we have been gathering nuances and connotations of the biblical words. We have gotten a general idea of what is involved.

Now we take a jump. We are not just interested in individual worship. We want to know what it means for the church to worship. So we are looking at the church.

So far, worship has been a very large concept for us. We have intentionally flung open the doors and kept them wide. And we have been learning that worship relates to just about every aspect of our relationship with God. It must be the same with the church. How does the church relate to God? Could it be that just about everything the church does is, in some way, *worship?*

We'll see . . . as we continue to flip through this photo album.

Acts 2 starts with a duplicate shot from Acts 1. "They were all together [*homothumadon*] in one place." Then the bomb hit. The Holy Spirit rushed in like a mighty wind. The Holy Spirit descended on each of them, looking like "tongues of fire." It was like the fire that danced about the "burning bush" as God spoke to Moses in the desert. It was like that cloud of fire—God's presence—that led Israel through the wilderness. It was like that fire that dropped into the Holy of Holies when Solomon dedicated the temple (remember that the disciples were probably in the temple complex). Except now it was split up and distributed among the believers. In a way, it must have looked like the bright dove that descended upon Jesus at his baptism, only now the brightness hovered over each Christian. It is not hard to decipher this picture: God is present with his people. This was the gift they had been waiting for.

What happened when the Spirit came? They talked. The believers "declared the wonders of God" (Acts 2:11). When the Spirit fills Christians, they erupt in praise.

Scholars have debated the logistics of Acts 2 for years. Were there just 12 speaking in tongues or 120? Were they speaking in the particular languages mentioned or in some heavenly language that the Spirit mysteriously translated into the native languages of the people present? Why was this language outbreak necessary, since virtually all of the Jews who were visiting Jerusalem for Pentecost would have spoken both Aramaic and Greek?

Let the scholars debate. Just notice two effects of this event. First, the tongues-speaking was a *sign* that drew people's attention and indicated that God was doing something special. Throughout the Book of Acts, tongues-speaking has this effect. Second, the tongues-speaking *communicated* the "wonders of God." There was content. It was not just "Hey, look at us!" but "Hey, listen to this!" In fact, the sign pointed to the communication. Not only did the people hear the disciples miraculously proclaim the wonders of God, they also stuck around for Peter's sermon.

Here is the third thing to notice: *Peter preached Jesus.* This was the gospel pure and simple: Jesus came from God, died, rose again; he is Lord. Scholars call this the *kerygma,* the central message of Christianity, the germ of the gospel. Spirit-filled worship testifies about Jesus.

Some may make the distinction that this was an evangelistic sermon, not really a worship service. It goes in the category of evangelism, not worship. Maybe so. But what do we see in this picture? The church gathers; the Spirit arrives and immediately makes things happen—including both the praise of God and the story of Jesus. The sermon has an evangelistic effect, obviously. Three thousand turn to Christ that day. And it is clear that Peter was trying to persuade his audience.

Does this mean that all our worship services should be evangelistic? Yes and no. Spirit-filled worship is evangelistic by nature. We may not have to try to make it so. The Spirit moves Christians to "declare the wonders of God" and these wonders include the story of Jesus. When unbelievers hear this story, it has an evangelistic effect. Worship and evangelism—at least in this snapshot—seem to knit together.

Our next snapshot comes in the aftermath of Pentecost. The church was off and running. Three thousand converts already and more every day. Many of these were probably pilgrims in Jerusalem who would have returned to their homelands. Other pilgrims might have stayed to learn more about this Christianity.

So what was the church doing? If they printed a church newsletter and listed "activities for the week," what would it say?

Luke listed four activities and (I believe) comments on them. "They devoted themselves to the apostles' teaching and to the fellowship, to the breaking of bread and to prayer." They had two worship places, the temple and their homes. (This would have been true of most Jews in Jerusalem. They would attend temple services and also observe family rituals at home.) The first two activities Luke mentioned seem to occur at the temple. The others would happen at various home meetings.

The apostles' teaching. Obviously, the apostles taught what Jesus had taught them. This probably consisted of explaining the Hebrew Scriptures in light of Jesus. How did he fulfill the prophecies? This is the way Jesus himself taught (Luke 24:27), and Peter followed his example at Pentecost (Acts 2:31). But, as at Pentecost, the teaching was probably accompanied by miracles, as happened in Acts 3. Peter and John healed a lame man, a crowd gathered, and Peter preached about Jesus. This was God's way of showing his approval, of validating their teaching. As Luke commented, "Everyone was filled with awe, and many wonders and miraculous signs were done by the apostles."

The King James Version used the expression "the apostles' doctrine," and this might suggest systematic theology and seven-point sermons on supralapsarianism. But it wasn't like that at all. We have the content of the apostles' teaching in the early chapters of Acts. They simply told Jesus' story—who he was, what he did. Remember that the church was at least 96 percent brand-new Christians. They needed the basics. They probably also needed the miraculous signs to keep reassuring them that this was God's teaching.

The fellowship. To us American Christians, this smacks of potluck dinners, right? Or at least a coffee hour after the morning service. As we see fellowship, it is a time to get to know each other, to be friends. But the biblical term is much, much stronger. The Greek word is *koinonia,* which means "commonness."

As Luke commented, "All the believers were together [*homothumadon*] and had everything in common." There is that phrase again—"with one accord." The last two times we saw this word, the believers were gathered together in one place (probably at the temple), praying. Luke wrote, "Every day they continued to meet together in the temple courts." Their numbers had grown. They spilled out, perhaps, from a side room to the open courts of the temple complex. But they continued to meet together for prayer. The fact that they had this prayer meeting at the temple suggests that they were following the Jewish rituals. There was a regular temple liturgy in which a priest would lead in prayers at certain times of day. Acts 3, for instance, begins with Peter and John going up to the temple "at the time of prayer—at three in the afternoon." It is likely that the Christians met at these times, followed the Jewish liturgies, and then broke off into a time of business and prayer of their own.

What business? Well, earlier we saw the church of 120 selecting a twelfth apostle. Here in Acts 2 we find more business to conduct. "Selling their possessions and goods, they gave to anyone as he had need." Many of the new believers would be needy, especially those who had not returned home from their Pentecost pilgrimage. Even some of the local converts might have been thrown out of their homes or jobs for associating with this "Jesus cult." And remember that most of the apostles themselves were Galileans, away from their home and livelihood. With three thousand-plus newborn Christians on their doorstep, there were lots of mouths to fill. Of course, some of the new converts would have been well-to-do. As Barnabas did later (Acts 4:36-37), these would have liquidated some of their assets and shared them with the poor believers. This too is involved in the "commonness," the koinonia fellowship of the early church.

The breaking of bread. Here we move out of the temple and into people's homes. "The breaking of bread" was originally a term for eating any meal, but very quickly the church latched onto the term for the Lord's Supper. All the Gospel writers record that, at his Last Supper, Jesus "took bread and broke it." He also commanded his disciples to repeat this meal to commemorate his own sacrifice for them.

The Last Supper was probably a Passover meal. In Jesus' time, just like today, this was a family ritual, a meal built around a liturgy, blessing God and commemorating the Jews' escape from Egypt. Certain prayers and blessings were to be said at certain times. At his last Passover, Jesus gave this ritual new meaning. As he raised the third cup of wine, after dinner, the cup of blessing, he was supposed to thank God for being true to his covenant with Israel. But instead (or in addition) he said, "This cup is the new covenant in my blood, which is poured out for you" (Luke 22:20). For his disciples, this ritual would never be the same.

If it was, in fact, a Passover meal, the disciples had a problem. It would be sacrilege to observe the Passover meal at any other time than Passover. They would have to wait a year before following Jesus' command to "do this in remembrance of me." But there was another tradition in Judaism, the Sabbath meal. A family would gather on the evening of each Sabbath and observe a lesser liturgy, but still thank God for his blessings. It seems as if the early Christians decided to observe this meal each week as their special devotion to Christ. Christians would invite others to their homes (especially those who did not live in Christian homes themselves) and share this meal in memory of Christ. Based on the Jewish model, there would be Scripture reading, prayer, and singing, along with the meal itself.

Prayer. We have already talked about prayer in the temple, which was probably more formal in nature, as part of the "fellowship" of the Christians. This mention of prayer probably has to do with informal prayer meetings in people's homes—possibly associated with the Lord's Supper, but perhaps held much more often. Farther down, Luke characterized the Christians eating "with glad and sincere hearts, praising God." The word for "sincere" can mean "simple." This may refer to the informality of these occasions. Perhaps prayers at the temple meetings were voiced by more polished leaders. These home rituals and prayers were more simple, emanating from the glad hearts of the participants.

We see one home prayer meeting in Acts 12. In the house of Mary, Mark's mother, "Many people had gathered and were praying" for Peter's release from prison. Then Peter showed up. Talk about effective prayer!

Many preachers have used this section of Acts 2 as an outline for the church's activity today. We should devote ourselves, they say, to teaching God's Word, fellowshipping with each other, worship ("breaking of bread" equals the sacraments or ordinances and that stands for all we do in our worship services), and prayer. They would skim through their church bulletin and point out the Sunday school time for teaching (as well as the sermon), the "fellowship time" before or after the service, the Sunday morning worship service, and the Wednesday night prayer meeting.

This makes some sense, but I don't like to see worship put in a box like that. It seems to me that all of these activities are aspects of worship. We come together on a Sunday morning to hear God's Word, to bring our gifts to be shared with those in need, to observe the ordinances as Christ commanded, and to pray together. It all flows from our relationship with God; it all reflects our response to God. We relate to each other in the process, but this is because we relate first to God. ("We love because he first loved us.") Thus I would see this snapshot in Acts 2, not as a smorgasbord of varied church activity, but as a full expression of Spirit-filled worship.

EIGHT
MORE SNAPSHOTS
(ACTS 4-8)

As the Book of Acts continues, we find more of the same. The Christians meet in the temple and in their homes. They pray and share their goods. The apostles work miracles and preach about Jesus.

Luke shows us one prayer meeting immediately after Peter and John were released from official custody: "They raised their voices together in prayer to God" (Acts 4:24). And the text follows with six-and-a-half verses of prayer—including praise, Scripture quoting, and pleas for strength.

But we come back to our previous questions about this corporate prayer. How did this work? If you were making a film about this event, how would you script it?

Back in Acts 1:14, we were merely told they "joined together in prayer." Here in Acts 4 we have what they said. The fact that they "raised their voices" further indicates that this was not just silent prayer. But was this a prayer that someone wrote down and everyone repeated? Probably not, because of the immediacy of the situation. Peter and John had just reported their experiences, and "when they heard this," the people prayed. Was this a prayer one person voiced and the others affirmed by saying, "Amen"? Possibly, but the text says, "*They* raised their voices together . . . *they* prayed." This may indicate that one person prayed a sentence at a time and the congregation repeated it (a form that various church traditions have used through the centuries). Or perhaps these are shreds of "sentence prayers" spoken by the people. When you analyze the prayer, it is not as smooth as a prepared prayer might be. You can almost hear one person praising, another quoting Scripture, another commenting on the fulfillment of that Scripture, and so on.

Flip the page to another snapshot. You might call this a "negative." Ananias and Sapphira sell some land. They pretend to give all of it to the church, but keep part of it for themselves. For this deceit they are struck dead. Luke recorded it in Acts 5.

Before we consider the moral of the story, let us look at some logistics. We should assume that the church is still meeting regularly at some place in the temple complex. Public teaching and healing happen out in the temple courts and in Solomon's Colonnade (Acts 5:12). They were also meeting in various houses (Acts 5:42), but would any homes be big enough to accommodate the entire church? No, the auxiliary rooms of the temple complex would serve this purpose best.

The way Luke spoke of placing gifts "at the apostles' feet" implies that the apostles presided at certain meetings of the entire church. Perhaps this gift-giving was part of the regular order of service. People would bring their offerings, not to the altar as in temple worship, but to the front of the assembly, trusting the apostles to use these funds for the care of the poor. Many churches today collect the offering in a similar way, not passing plates, but inviting givers to bring their gifts forward.

So it appears that Ananias made his gift in a public way, announcing that, like Barnabas and others, he had sold land and was donating the entire proceeds. His wife, Sapphira, came in "about three hours later." The times of prayer at the temple were nine o'clock, three o'clock, and sunset, and the church may have followed this pattern for its meetings. So Ananias may have made the gift at the afternoon service and Sapphira showed up at sunset.

Whatever, both were struck dead. The Bible contains other stories of swift divine judgment, and this report bears some resemblance to the account of Achan's sin in Joshua 7. The Israelites had just entered the Promised Land and had conquered Jericho in miraculous fashion. Joshua declared, "The city and all that is in it are to be devoted to the Lord" (Josh. 6:17). That is, all the metals—silver, gold, bronze, and iron—would be brought back to the tabernacle treasury. All the perishable goods, tainted by Jericho's paganism, would be burned. But one soldier, Achan, saw a beautiful Babylonian robe, some silver coins, and a bar of gold. These he grabbed and hid under his tent, thinking that no one would know.

The Israelite army then attempted to take the tiny town of Ai but suffered a miserable defeat. Why? Someone had "held back [the Greek translation of Josh. 7:1 has *nosphizo*—remember this word] the devoted things." Eventually Achan was pinpointed and stoned to death.

Like Achan, Ananias and Sapphira stood at the beginning of a great new thing God was doing for his people. In both cases, God needed to set precedent. Like Achan, Ananias "held back" (the same word, *nosphizo*) from the Lord and yet tried to continue as if nothing was wrong. Both were challenged face to face by the leaders of God's people (Joshua and Peter). And both were judged swiftly.

But consider this crime of "holding back." Peter made clear that Ananias and Sapphira didn't have to give all the money from the land. "Wasn't the money at your disposal?" he asked. There is nothing wrong with holding back something that is yours. (The only other biblical use of *nosphizo* is in Titus 2:10, where slaves are urged not to "hold back" from their masters. It can mean "steal" in this case, but it may also refer to faithful effort. Slaves "belong," not to themselves, but to their masters and thus owe them an honest day's work and should not hold back.)

But when Ananias declared that he was giving the entire price of the land to the Lord, that price became a "devoted thing." It belonged to the Lord. And so he was "holding back."

The Acts text announced that Ananias and Sapphira lied to the Lord. This was their sin. If they hadn't lied, everything would be fine. If they had said, "Peter, here is half the money from our real estate deal. We're putting the rest in a retirement account," Peter may have chided them for not trusting the Lord for their retirement, but at least they might have lived that long. But they falsely claimed to be more devoted than they were. And this meant they were holding back.

What would have made them lie like that? Peter was asking the same question (Acts 5:4). All he could figure was that Satan had filled Ananias's heart. But filled it with what? What would this couple gain by lying? Respect, maybe.

Perhaps they wanted to be considered major financial benefactors of the church. This would bring all sorts of fringe benefits. They might get the front-row seats. They could hobnob with the apostles. This still goes on today as Christian media ministries curry favor with rich donors. James indicated that it happened in the early church, too. He

67

pictured a man entering the church meeting "wearing a gold ring and fine clothes" (James 2:1-4). This man is shown special attention and offered a good seat, while a poor man "in shabby clothes" is ignored. Ananias and Sapphira may have craved this attention.

Or maybe they wanted to be considered as "spiritual" as Barnabas. Barnabas, we know, had a great reputation in the early church, primarily as an encourager. He had donated the proceeds of a land sale to the church. They could gain a similar reputation with such a show of charity. Or so they may have thought.

The fact is, they didn't trust God enough to let him have all the money from their land. But they wanted people to think they were that trusting. The problem was not simply that they lacked trust. God knows that people need to grow in their faith. He doesn't punish them for not being farther along in the growing process. But Ananias and Sapphira were faking it. And that was wrong. Dead wrong!

So what do we learn about worship here? Worship must never be used by us to further our own reputations. We must never try to show people through our worship that we are more "spiritual" than we really are. We must be honest with the Lord and with the church—even if that means admitting our shortcomings.

Gulp.

What do we see in our churches? Honesty? In far too many, Sunday morning is a sham. We dress in our Sunday best to hide our weekday worst. We smile at those we were gossiping about yesterday, and we pretend we have no sin.

The great British expositor G. Campbell Morgan commented,

> If a man attends a convention or a religious service and sings with fervor, "My all is on the altar," when it is not, he is committing the sin of Ananias and Sapphira. The church's administration today is not what it was, or there might be many dead men and women at the end of some services. The sin of Ananias and Sapphira is that of attempting, by confession of the mouth, or song of the lips, to make it appear that things are as they really are not.[1]

One of the biggest problems nonchurchgoers have with churchgoing is hypocrisy. We are all hypocrites, they say, judging others when we're just as bad. Too often, they are right. How amazing, then, that Jesus saved his most scathing rebukes, not for the immoral folks that we rail against, but for the hypocrites. And five chapters into the Book of Acts, the same lesson is made painfully clear: Be real. Don't lie to God.

As the church grew, its activity increased. Part of its ministry involved distributing food to widows who had no families to care for them. There was some bickering going on, and the apostles found themselves spending far too much time on the administration of this program and not enough on preaching and prayer. As they put it, "It would not be right for us to neglect the ministry of the word of God in order to wait on tables." If you have ever been in a growing church, you know how this is. When the pastor is spending all day typing letters and fixing the copier, it is time to hire a secretary.

The early church needed deacons. They chose seven men who were "full of the Spirit and wisdom." These were lofty qualifications for people who were going to "wait on tables," but the church took this task seriously.

We find here the church's first "division of labor." Later, Paul made a theology out of it. We are a body, he said. Some are eyes, some ears, some feet. We all can't do everything. But up to this point, the apostles were trying to do everything, and they were probably burning out.

We generally assume that the deacons were subordinate to the apostles, that they were "helpers," assigned to do the dirty work while the apostles stayed with the important stuff. But this was not necessarily the case. Later in church history, deacons are clearly subordinate to elders and overseers, but this may not have been the original intent.

Note the exceptional qualifications of these men. The task they were given carried great authority—they managed the financial resources of the young church. And we see two of these deacons, Stephen and Philip, go on to minister in similar ways as the apostles.

The division of labor makes sense for several reasons. First, the apostles had been taught by Jesus himself. Thus they would be the better teachers of the church, passing on a firsthand account of Jesus' teaching. Second, the apostles were probably all on one side of the Hebraic-Grecian controversy. The Grecian Jews (probably those who had come from other countries for Pentecost, were converted, and settled in Jerusalem; their culture would have been more Greek than Hebrew) had complained that they were being overlooked, that the Hebraic Jews were getting a bigger slice of the church pie. The apostles, Hebraic themselves, may have recognized their blind spot. Interestingly, the seven deacons all have Greek names, and include one

Greek convert to Judaism. The Grecian widows couldn't complain anymore.

But there is no indication that the distribution of food was of any lesser importance than the ministry of the Word. It was just becoming more time-consuming. All of this ministry was important. The apostles needed to bring on more staff members to handle it all.

To our modern minds, it seems that this division of labor put the apostles in charge of "worship" and the deacons in charge of "ministry." But remember Luke's summary at the end of Acts 2 and our attempt to see it all as worship. The church assembled in the temple and in homes for teaching, fellowship (which included the collecting and distribution of goods), breaking of bread (the Lord's Supper), and prayer (both collectively in temple services and more informally in homes). Now the apostles decide to concentrate on the teaching and collective prayer. They turn the "fellowship" over to the deacons. And, most likely, the Lord's Supper and informal prayers are already being led by various house-church leaders.

A few more brief glimpses in Acts will catapult us into the Epistles and early church history. Acts 8:1 grimly records a great persecution that "broke out against the church at Jerusalem, and all except the apostles were scattered throughout Judea and Samaria."

Jesus had announced earlier that his followers would be witnesses "in Jerusalem, and in all Judea and Samaria, and to the ends of the earth" (Acts 1:8). Like ripples in a pond, the church would spread out. Here are the second and third ripples, motivated by persecution.

Obviously, the church could no longer meet in the temple courts. It was too dangerous. They could still meet in homes, however, wherever persecution might drive them. This decentralized the church. The apostles stayed in Jerusalem for several years yet, as a resource, as a central governing body. But the action was happening in numerous homes in Damascus and Antioch and, increasingly, throughout the Mediterranean world.

Our next snapshot comes from Corinth. The church had continued to ripple outward. The assembly at Antioch had sent Paul and Barnabas off on one church-planting journey through Asia Minor, and now Paul was taking a second trip, this one into Greece. In a previous chapter we saw Paul preaching to the Athenian philosophers. Next he went across the isthmus to Corinth, where he entrenched himself for a while, living with Priscilla and Aquila and joining their tentmaking business. "Every Sabbath he reasoned in the synagogue, trying to persuade Jews and Greeks" (Acts 18:4).

As we have already seen, synagogues existed throughout the Roman Empire, wherever there were pockets of Jewish immigrants. In the "anything goes" spirituality of that time, many Gentiles were attracted to the Jews' monotheism and moral structure. These "God-worshipers" would attend synagogue services, where there would be prayers, songs, Scripture reading, and explanation of the Scripture. Synagogues had a custom of welcoming traveling rabbis, so Paul (with his extensive Jewish credentials) would often be invited to speak. This became his custom (Acts 14:1) as he visited various cities. He would go first to the synagogue and try "to persuade Jews and Greeks."

In Corinth, as elsewhere, Paul eventually met opposition from Orthodox Jews. He announced, "Your blood be on your own heads! I am clear of my responsibility. From now on I will go to the Gentiles."

Then Paul left the synagogue and began to preach next door, at the home of a Greek God-worshiper, Titius Justus. Presumably the home was large enough to accommodate the "many" Corinthians who were converted through Paul's ministry there.

This picture gives us a pattern for Paul's ministry. In Ephesus, he preached in the synagogue over a three-month period but was eventually forced out. "He took the disciples with him and had discussions daily in the lecture hall of Tyrannus" (Acts 19:9).

In Corinth, Ephesus, and many other cities, the church was made up of people who had first heard the gospel in a synagogue service—not just once, but over months and months. Thus the prayers and songs and Scriptures of the synagogue service would have become imbued with Christian meaning, as Paul would take the preaching time to explain the Hebrew Scriptures in light of Jesus.

This means that the first Christian worship services in these areas were Jewish worship services.

So what would happen when the church moved next door, or down the street? They would maintain most of the synagogue forms of worship: prayers, singing, Scripture reading, and preaching. There was one exception: the Lord's Supper. This is a distinctively Christian form of worship that would not have been practiced in the synagogue. But, just as it was in Jerusalem, the Lord's Supper would probably continue to be observed in individual homes. Paul probably practiced it each week with Priscilla and Aquila and any other new Christian believers from the synagogue they might invite. Most likely, they did this on Sunday, the day of Jesus' resurrection.

We get one indication of this from a strange event in Troas. As Luke described it, "On the first day of the week we came together to break bread." Breaking bread, you recall, is Luke's term for the Lord's Supper. They apparently were meeting on Sunday to do this. Paul had stayed in Troas for a week and was leaving the next day, so he spoke at length to the people.

At great length!

Well, about midnight, one of the teenagers sitting by a window fell asleep—and fell. Three stories. (Once again, the Christians were meeting in an "upper room," but we don't know whether it was a house or some assembly hall.) Although the young man died in the fall, Paul picked him up and raised him to life. Then everyone went back upstairs where they "broke bread and ate." That is, they observed the Lord's Supper and then they had their fellowship meal, what became known as a "love feast." (More on this in the next chapter.)

So, we have seen the church's photo album. What impression do we get?

Let me suggest that we are looking at a church not built on form but on energy. The power of the Holy Spirit flows through these people and drives them:

Out to tell others.

Together to share the Lord's Supper.

Forward to lay their belongings at the apostles' feet.

To the temple or synagogue to hear the apostles' teaching.

"From house to house" to pray together.

The forms of worship the church chooses come from various sources, but the Spirit flows through them all to make them his own.

Notes

1. G. Campbell Morgan, *The Acts of the Apostles* (Old Tappan, N.J.: Revell, 1924), 148-9.

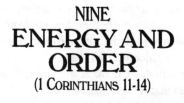

NINE
ENERGY AND ORDER
(1 CORINTHIANS 11-14)

Let's invent a religion.

How do we go about it? What do we make up first?

Most people would establish a set of rituals right away. Here is how to pray. Here is how to sit or stand. Here are the words to say. Here is the secret handshake.

But Christianity is not like that. In fact, that is one of the frustrations that scholars face in trying to find out how the early church worshiped. The New Testament, by and large, does not tell us these things. Sitting, standing, singing the first and last verses of slow hymns, when to give the announcements. It is as if these things don't matter much.

Apart from a few instructions about the Lord's Supper, and possibly the Lord's Prayer, the founding documents of the church do not stipulate worship forms.

They do, however, critique the spirit of worship. The first converts worshiped "with gladness and sincerity of heart"; Ananias and Sapphira had a lying spirit; the Corinthians (as we will see) were greedy and impatient.

Forms were available to them. They had a few ordinances established by Jesus. Much could be borrowed from Jewish worship. And the Roman Empire was rife with mystery cults that had secret rites and banquets and sacrifices. If the church so chose, even these forms could be used in the service of God. But the distinction of Christianity was in its spirit. When he warned his flock about false teachers, John did

73

not say, "Check out their liturgies to see if they do things right." He said, "Test the spirits to see whether they are from God" (1 John 4:1, NIV). The forms were just clothes that the church in its spirit of worship put on. Some fit very nicely, others didn't.

This does not mean that Christian worship is formless. Many Christians have the idea that it is enough to stare blankly into space, as long as their attitude is "worshipful." No, remember that "spiritual" in its biblical use does not mean nonphysical. It means a body that is controlled by the Spirit. When the Spirit is active in your life, your body is active, too. The Spirit is your energy, your battery pack, motivating your actions.

And when your spirit is not in tune with God's Spirit, it results in bad actions—even in worship. That is where we find the Corinthians.

We saw how the Corinthian church started in the synagogue. Some leading Jews of that city accepted Christ through Paul's teaching. Crispus, formerly the synagogue ruler (Acts 18:8), was probably a leader in the church by now. We saw how opposition arose, chasing the church next door to the house of Titius Justus. We don't know much about Justus, except that he had a Roman name and a house big enough to hold the church assembly. Was he perhaps a wealthy trader from Rome, or some government bureaucrat? The church may still have been meeting in his home when Paul wrote. Another church member we should mention is Stephanas. At the end of this letter, Paul hailed this Greek man as the first Christian convert in that part of Greece (1 Cor. 16:15-18). The way Paul begged the Corinthians to show respect for Stephanas suggests that he may have been a church leader who was fighting factions within the church. Stephanas had just visited Paul in Ephesus. In fact, he may have carried with him the list of questions that Paul answered in this epistle (and he might have carried back this letter).

The church was divided. Some were claiming to follow Peter, others Paul, or that Alexandrian upstart, Apollos. When you consider that we have already met a prominent Jew, a Roman, and a Greek, that is not surprising. The factions may have followed racial lines.

And yet Paul didn't take a lot of time discussing how Jesus had united Jews and Gentiles (as he did in other epistles). The divisions weren't theological—they were practical, behavioral. Should I eat meat offered to idols? Should Christians take each other to court? Is it all right for Christians to marry? How harsh should we be in punishing a sinning church member?

74

No doubt, the different groups took different positions on these matters. It was not so much a matter of racial prejudice but more of conflicting traditions.

Many a marriage has struggled with conflicting traditions. He expects her to take out the trash; that is part of the "woman's work" his mom always did. She expects him to take out the trash; her dad always did. Even something as trivial as trash can spark a major battle. Why? Because both people's expectations, assumptions, and images of marriage are wrapped up (so to speak) in this simple act. "If he loved me, he would . . . " "If she loved me, she would . . . "

One of our greatest statements of understanding these days is, "I know where you're coming from." It is not just knowing what you think or how you feel. It is understanding your traditions—why you think and feel as you do.

The Gentile Corinthians came out of an idol-worshiping culture. The thought of eating meat that had been offered in sacrifices to idols bothered some of them. Deep down inside, it offended them, either because a Christian had no business participating in anything related to idols or because they still had a sense of the evil spiritual power involved in idol worship.

Jews had no such problem. The meat was cheap. Those "gods" had no real power. Why not?

They were "coming from" totally different angles.

This becomes very important when we consider worship—both in 1 Corinthians and in the modern church. People now, as then, have their traditions. They may know in their heads that there is nothing unscriptural about, say, clapping their hands along with a hymn—but it bothers them. Where they are coming from, that is not worship.

The Corinthians' first worship question (1 Cor. 11:2-16) involved dress code. Should men cover their heads in worship? Should women?

This is a puzzling passage, deeply rooted in the culture of Corinth. We will deal with it here only briefly, but I believe we can learn a few things about worship.

Paul said men should not cover their heads in worship. Traditionally, Jewish men have worn hats, veils, or yarmulkes in synagogue worship as a sign of reverence. Probably, before this letter, most of the Jewish Christian men were covering their heads. Some would have been upset that the Gentile men did not. Didn't they have respect for God?

75

This was a traditional thing again. A Gentile might answer, "Sure I have respect for God, but I show it in other ways. Get off my back!"

Knowing the Corinthian church as we do, it is not hard to surmise that the head-coverers began to group together as a separate faction, complaining that the bareheads lacked spirituality.

This had to stop, Paul said. He was primarily concerned about church unity. Everyone should do one thing or the other. (Unity does not always mean uniformity, but in this case the different styles had become politicized.) Should he require everyone to wear hats? No. That would set a bad precedent. He would be making everyone "Jewish," at least as far as haberdashery was concerned. This was something he fought throughout his whole career. Many Jewish Christians were trying to Judaize the Gentiles, demanding that they be circumcised and follow Old Testament law. Paul insisted that Christianity was something new: Gentiles did not have to follow Jewish tradition. Together they would forge a new tradition.

As Paul thought about it, the head covering seemed to reflect a limitation in the Jewish faith. Reverence is fine, but so often the traditions seemed to block the way to God, rather than move us closer. The law was supposed to lead us to Christ (Gal. 3:24), but as it was practiced, it got in the way.

In Christ, believers have access to God. We are not only created in his image (Gen. 1:27), we are remade in his image, as God makes us more and more like Christ. We are his glory. God enjoys being with us as we worship him. We ourselves are the shining examples of his power and love.

And therefore, Paul said, the hats don't make sense. They separate us from God. Almost in a physical sense, they bottle up our praises inside our heads, keeping us from the full and open expression of our worship. Jewish worship may have been about reverence, but Christian worship is about open fellowship with God.

We have to switch gears when we move to women's head coverings. There was still a cultural problem, but this was with the Greek culture, not the Jewish. For a woman to uncover her head in public was immodest. She would look like a loose woman, even a prostitute. Paul might even be afraid that the worshiping men might be distracted by the unveiled women.

So why did this have to be said? Some of the women may have been flouting the conventions of the day. You can hear them saying, "Why should we worry about what others think? We women have open access to God, too. We have freedom in the church to worship however we like."

But the church had to be above reproach. Other Greek religions had temple prostitutes and sexual rites. Christianity had to be different— and let everyone know that. Already, women were more involved in the church than in other religions of that time. It would be easy for an observer to get the wrong idea. Christians talked of loving each other; they even had "love feasts"; and they greeted each other with kisses (Rom. 16:16). They preached freedom in Christ. You didn't have to observe that restrictive Hebrew law anymore.

The New Testament offers plentiful evidence that sexual temptation was all around the church—and even within it. Some of the heresies that afflicted the early church would involve sexual immorality (Rev. 2:20-24). The Corinthian church itself had been winking at an inces- tuous affair within its ranks. Christians had to be careful.

So here, as elsewhere (1 Tim. 2:9-10), Paul urged women to adorn themselves modestly when they came to worship.

A few principles emerge in this passage:

1. It matters how worship looks. The way we look as we worship reflects certain things about the nature of what we are doing. Head covering means something, so we should be careful about the forms and styles we choose.

2. Christianity does not have to cater to non-Christian ideas of how to worship. We are doing a different thing.

3. Yet we do need to be sensitive to non-Christian ideas, in order to avoid creating a wrong impression of who we are. (For instance, some churches make a point of asking visitors not to put money in the offering plate. There's nothing wrong with giving, but in our modern culture, many people think the church is only out for money. Thus, in the spirit of 1 Corinthians 11, these churches have altered what is otherwise a very noble and harmless tradition—just so outsiders won't get the wrong idea.)

The Corinthians had a second problem in worship: the Lord's Supper. They were messing it up to the point that their meetings were doing "more harm than good" (1 Cor. 11:17).

Apparently the "breaking of bread" that the early church began to observe on a regular basis (Acts 2:42) was a full meal. Early Christian literature calls this the "love feast" or sometimes just the *agape*. Just as the Jewish Passover integrated prayers, blessings, and songs into the dinner, so the church remembered Jesus.

Originally, the bread was broken at the beginning of the meal—with the appropriate words concerning Christ's body. Then, after dinner, the cup of wine was taken, symbolizing Christ's blood. In between, of course, was the meal. At a church gathering like this one in Corinth, it would be "potluck," with various members bringing various courses and sharing. It is possible that Scripture was read during the meal, with songs and exhortations—essentially a church service conducted as the people ate. (In the second century, however, the *agape* feast was separate from the major time of worship and instruction.)

But those Corinthians were doing it wrong. "It is not the Lord's supper that you eat," Paul scolded. He used a curious form here: "Lordly" supper, we might say, or "Lordlike." It is not in keeping with what the Lord has taught.

Each family or clique was bringing its own food and not waiting for anyone else. They were not sharing with the poor as they should. People were "pigging out" and getting drunk. This is behavior you might expect from the cults.

Various pagan religions and cult groups in the Roman Empire held banquets. These would be festive times of wining and dining and sometimes sexual immorality—with a few religious rituals thrown in. This may be why Paul spoke as he did: "This may be all right for Apollo's supper or Dionysius's feast, but it doesn't befit the Lord Jesus."

Paul mentioned divisions again. Maybe this was another Jew-Gentile thing. Some Jews would avoid eating certain meats, so they would bring their own food and retreat to some corner where their group could dine in peace. Some others might bring meat that had been offered to idols. Others might have been vegetarian. As far as Paul was concerned, he didn't care what they ate, but their eating habits were dividing the church. What had been intended as a unified celebration of Christ was becoming a travesty.

After telling the story of the first Lord's Supper, the apostle gave explicit instructions. Examine yourself. Remember that this is the body and blood of the Lord you are partaking of. Wait for each other; eat together. And if you are too hungry to wait, eat at home.

The point is clear: The Lord's Supper is not about eating; it is about Jesus. We come together not to get filled up physically, but to commemorate Christ's death.

The church learned its lesson. History tells us that the love feast died out in the next century or so—maybe because of abuses like this.

Communion continued. The Eucharist remained a major part of the church's worship, as it is today. But it won't fill anybody up—physically, that is.

But we can learn other lessons here, too. I might go to church one Sunday and sit with my friends, avoiding those I don't like; I would check out what everyone was wearing; I would be critical of the choir because the song was so slow and boring; I would snicker at the assistant pastor's Scripture reading because he mispronounced "Mephibosheth"—I could have done much better; but I like the soloist's upbeat song (and besides, she's cute; maybe I can flirt with her later); and the guest speaker tells a lot of jokes, so he keeps my attention; I hobnob with the right people on the way out; and I leave with the feeling that I really "got something out of" this church service.

But whose service was this? I can almost hear Paul saying, "It's not the Lord's worship you attended." It may have been entertaining or socially satisfying. It might be fine for the theater or health club. But the church's worship service is not about entertainment or scoring points with friends. It is about Jesus. Do we really "recognize the Lord" (1 Cor. 11:29) in this service?

Next problem: spiritual gifts. Are some gifts better than others? Are they all from the Spirit? How can we tell who should do what?

In 1 Corinthians 12, Paul discussed spiritual gifts at length. Although we usually don't think of this chapter in connection with worship, we should. Chapters 11 and 14 discuss matters of public worship, why not chapter 12? Look briefly at Paul's main points.

1. Spiritual gifts affirm Jesus' lordship (v. 3). There will be phonies, claiming spiritual empowerment for various "spiritual" manifestations. But only the Holy Spirit can say, "Jesus is Lord."

2. Spiritual gifts come from the same Spirit, and thus should foster church unity (vv. 4-6). Christianity is not a cookie-cutter religion. God doesn't want clones. He gives out varied gifts—but this diversity should reflect back to his unity.

3. Spiritual gifts are a public matter (v. 7). They are "for the common good." No one should use his gift to exalt himself or put down others.

There follows a list of spiritual gifts. It is not comprehensive. We find other such lists in Ephesians 4 and Romans 12. But let me suggest that these are gifts specifically for use in Christian worship.

The message of wisdom may have to do with church leadership. (Wisdom was a major requirement for the church's first deacons in

Acts 6.) God would give to the church leaders a message that said, "This is what the church should do," and this message would be delivered during the church's worship gatherings.

The message of knowledge is probably a gift of teaching, also used in public worship. (Some might distinguish here between teaching and preaching. The message of wisdom might correspond to a preaching ministry that would apply the message of knowledge to the church's situation. The teacher conveys the knowledge of what the Scripture says, while the preacher imparts the wisdom of what it means for us.)

Faith, healing, and miraculous powers may go together. James wrote, "The prayer offered in faith [literally, the prayer of faith] will make the sick person well" (James 5:15). The person with the gift of faith may be a prayer leader, who is given knowledge of what to pray for along with the confidence that God will answer. Healing may or may not be miraculous. Even in early centuries, Christians were known as care-givers and often hired as nurses. Yet, at the very start of the church, miraculous healing was a part of the Christians' meetings in the temple (Acts 5:12-16). This may have continued in the church worship services, though Scripture is rather quiet about it.

Prophecy and distinguishing between spirits work together. Acts indicates that various prophets functioned in the early church, giving special words from the Lord. Yet fakery quickly became a problem. Anyone could stand up and say, "The Lord told me that you should raise a million denarii and buy me a villa on Capri." Thus the New Testament urges Christians to "test the spirits to see whether they are from God" (1 John 4:1). Demonic spirits would not affirm the lordship of Christ. Yet the church needed a separate gift, the ability to determine whether a "prophet" was actually giving God's message or just spouting off his own thoughts.

Tongues and interpretation of tongues also function in tandem in public worship. Paul wrote later in this epistle about tongues-speaking, giving some guidelines. But apparently at this time God gave certain people the ability to speak his praises in other languages (or in some heavenly language). And, just as the prophets needed a checkpoint, so the tongues-speakers needed an interpreter—so that the whole church could participate in their praises.

Paul made additional points about worship in the church. We have seen three already—we will pick up where we left off.

4. Spiritual gifts are interconnected, interdependent (vv. 12-31). In the brilliant analogy of the human body, Paul explained that all parts

of the church need the other parts. All gifts are important. The soloist is not more important than the usher. The pastor is not to be prized more than the nursery attendant.

5. Spiritual gifts are superseded by love (ch. 13). Those who exercise their spiritual gifts must do so with love. Think about what chapter 13 must have meant to the bickering Corinthians. We are used to seeing this written in gentle calligraphy and decoupaged onto wall plaques. But Paul was in the trenches, confronting real live problems. "Love is patient, love is kind. It does not envy, it does not boast, it is not proud." Think of that, you who claim to be wiser than the rest.

"It is not rude, it is not self-seeking." Remember that when you are wolfing down the Lord's Supper.

"It is not easily angered, it keeps no record of wrongs." You who want to take each other to court—are you listening?

All those gifts they were envying in each other don't mean a thing without this tremendous gift called love—*agape*, the thing they were supposed to be celebrating at their church feast.

6. Christian worship needs to involve the mind (14:6-19). Tongues-speaking and "singing in the spirit" were great spiritual and emotional experiences, but they weren't much help if no one else knew what was going on. Worship should be spiritual and mental. We need to communicate clearly with each other as we praise the Lord, so that they can say amen to our praises.

That amen-saying is crucial because it involves the whole church in corporate worship. It is not enough for each individual to have his or her own "worship experience," praying or singing in one's own spiritual reverie. We need to participate together in worship. Someone else may voice the praises, but I say amen and make the praises mine.

7. Christian worship exhibits the presence of God (14:22-25). Paul was concerned about visitors coming into the assembly and getting the wrong idea. Tongues-speaking, as a sign of God's power, may attract them initially, draw their interest. But if they enter our church and find us still muttering in strange languages, they will think we are crazy. If there is no sense to what we say, we lose them. There is no reason for them to stay. God may show his power through miraculous utterances, but he reveals his presence through intelligible words.

Other religions of that day had tongues-speaking. Priests or priestesses would work themselves into a frenzy and mouth strange syllables. It was a show of spiritual power. In the free-wheeling religious world of the first century, people were interested in bizarre phenomena (not unlike today). Someone would go into some spiritual trance, do something strange or miraculous, and you would take a look, check it out. In most cases it would be pretty disappointing—obvious fakery or nonsense or oppressive demonism.

God used the spiritual interest of the day to attract people to Christianity. But, once inside the church, seekers had to find something real. The "come-on" of tongues-speaking had to give way to something that could seriously change someone's life. And so Paul urged the Corinthians to "prophesy"—to speak forth the truths of God. This will lead seekers to repentance and make them say, "God is really among you!"

8. Christian worship is peaceful and orderly. People should not interrupt each other but allow each one to speak in turn. Even when someone is prophesying, empowered by God's Spirit, he should be able to control himself and wait for the previous speaker to finish—because God certainly wouldn't interrupt himself. "For God is not a God of disorder but of peace" (1 Cor. 14:33).

The word Paul used for disorder can mean "riot." Jesus used it to predict, "You [will] hear of wars and revolutions" (Luke 21:9). In a less political sense, James said, "For where you have envy and selfish ambition, there you find disorder and every evil practice" (James 3:16). That fits the Corinthian situation perfectly. James spoke of the wisdom from heaven that is "first of all pure, then peace-loving."

This passage is not saying that we need to follow a set order of service each week. Someone once quoted to me, "God is not a God of disorder but of order." That is not exactly right. The disorder Paul talked about has little to do with how well organized the service is; it does have to do with relations between people. God does not cause riots in the church. We should worship him together without fighting among ourselves. Paul told Timothy something similar: "I want men everywhere to lift up holy hands in prayer, without anger or disputing" (1 Tim. 2:8).

Paul gave us a capsule description of the church at worship in 1 Corinthians 14:26. "When you come together, everyone has a hymn, or a word of instruction, a revelation, a tongue or an interpretation." Everyone had something to offer to everyone else. Everyone had a gift to share.

Nowadays we tend to think that the pastor is responsible for creating the worship service. Perhaps the song leader or choir director would help. All we do is to sit and listen. But Scripture shows us a church in which everyone participates—maybe not up front, but at least saying amen.

I love going to my parents' church. In the middle of the service, they have a time of singing choruses—and then an open time of informal praise. One person quotes a Scripture verse. Another praises God. Another begins to sing a chorus of a well-known hymn, and the congregation joins in. As God leads, he is praised in all these ways.

Sometimes I think the Corinthian church must have been like that—on its better days.

TEN

THEY'RE PLAYING OUR SONG

(COLOSSIANS 2-3)

Music has a power all its own. It can make you laugh or cry, remember or forget. A middle-aged couple, out for a drive, will turn up the radio—"Listen, honey, they're playing our song." The music evokes memories of courtship, of romance. Feelings of love well up inside them as they listen again. (Someday couples will point to the TV set and say, "Look, honey, they're playing our video.")

People use songs to communicate with each other and to avoid communicating. The frustrated suitor writes ballads to woo his beloved, yet he may easily pass her on the street without noticing—he is lost in the sounds from his Walkman.

Music can lead you into worship or away from it.

My mother used to tell me of the thrill of singing "Wonderful Grace of Jesus" with a thousand others in her college chapel. And I remember singing "Fairest Lord Jesus" with the choir at that same college, hitting notes I didn't know I could hit.

God's people have always erupted in song to celebrate God's works and to thank him. Israel crossed the Red Sea and Moses led them in song, with Miriam leading the dance troupe with tambourines (Exod. 15). But singing also accompanied their worship of the golden calf (Exod. 32:18).

Deborah and Barak sang a victory duet (Judg. 5); and Hannah sang in thanksgiving for the birth of her son Samuel. David, the "sweet singer of Israel," calmed King Saul's manic heart with harp music

(1 Sam. 16:14-23), but it was the singing of David's followers that got him in trouble. "Saul has slain his thousands, and David his tens of thousands," the women sang after David's upset of Goliath. That made a jealous Saul use his young harpist for target practice. David, of course, wrote many majestic psalms of praise. But his experiences with Saul and other enemies inspired him to write plaintive psalms as well, things like: "O Lord, see how my enemies persecute me! Have mercy and lift me up from the gates of death."

In the first two chapters of his Gospel, Luke recorded highly poetic songs of Mary, Zechariah, the angels, and Simeon—all heralding the coming of the Messiah. Later, Paul and Silas sang psalms in a Philippian prison (Acts 16). Here and there throughout the epistles we find what seem to be shreds of hymn texts—for instance, the account of Christ's "emptying" and exaltation in Philippians 2. And, as we will see, the Book of Revelation is packed with songs of praise.

Small wonder then that Paul urges the Ephesians and the Colossians to "sing psalms, hymns and spiritual songs with gratitude in your hearts to God" (Col. 3:16; Eph. 5:19). Singing is quite appropriate for the church, when it is done with the proper attitude.

Psalms, hymns, and spiritual songs. Scholars disagree on just what those three types of music are. Psalms probably were the Old Testament psalms set to music. Hymns may have been original compositions that developed in the church. Spiritual songs may have been the spirit-led singing Paul mentioned briefly in 1 Corinthians 14:15.

There may have been some questions in Corinth as to what kind of songs were appropriate. Some denominations still sing only texts from the psalms. And many modern churches would have a hard time with the charismatic-style "singing in the spirit." But Paul seemed to be saying, "All of the above." Sing any kind of music, as long as it expresses your gratitude to God.

Music belongs in both personal and corporate worship. In Ephesians, Paul wrote more personally. "Speak to one another with psalms, hymns, and spiritual songs. Sing and make music in your heart to the Lord, always giving thanks." We support each other in the faith by singing to God. And a song of praise should be playing in our hearts, much like you would turn the radio on at work and listen throughout the day. So the thankful strains of God's praise should be a constant soundtrack for our lives.

But the Colossians passage puts music squarely in the center of corporate worship. In fact, Paul may be basing Colossians 2 and 3 on an actual worship service. It is as if he had a church bulletin from Colosse and was following along, making comments as he went.

Consider: It begins in Colossians 2:20. "Since you died with Christ." It is a baptismal service Paul was thinking about. Along with Communion, baptism was one of the church's earliest rituals. (Please don't get hung up here on the form of baptism. The early church did allow for pouring or sprinkling in certain circumstances, but I'm operating on the assumption that the Colossians immersed.) Even in biblical times, the meaning of baptism was clear. The one who was baptized was identifying with Christ in his death, burial, and resurrection. Christ's death "washes our sins away," and we rise with him, clean and new. So Paul began his commentary by urging the Colossians to let the old regulations of their past float away.

"Since, then, you have been raised with Christ, set your hearts on things above" (Col. 3:1). As the one being baptized comes up out of the water, it is a picture of resurrection. We are raised with Christ to newness of life. We should adopt a new perspective.

Continuing in the baptism mode, Paul spoke of taking off our old self and putting on the new self (Col. 3:9-10). People took off their clothes to be be baptized and put on fresh white robes afterward. Paul, possibly alluding to this, said, "Clothe yourselves with compassion, kindness, humility, gentleness, and patience" (Col. 3:12).

But I see shreds of a worship service in the following verses as well, as if Paul was envisioning the church service continuing after the baptism.

"Forgive as the Lord forgave you." Is this a reference to the Lord's Prayer? Jesus himself had made a similar comment about the prayer (Matt. 6:14). We pray, "Forgive us our debts," but as baptized believers—clean, new, fresh—we need to extend that same forgiveness to others.

"Let the peace of Christ rule in your hearts." Even today the "passing of the peace" exists in many church liturgies. People turn to each other with a kiss or hug or handshake and say, "The Peace of Christ be with you." "And also with you," comes the reply. This is an ancient tradition, going back to the New Testament. Paul told both the Romans and Corinthians, "Greet one another with a holy kiss" (Rom. 16:16; 2 Cor. 13:12). Paul may be have been observing this ritual and saying, "Make sure this peace isn't only on your lips but also inside you."

"And be thankful" (Col. 3:15) may be a brief reference to a particular prayer of thanks. Perhaps as the preacher lifted the Scriptures to read them, the congregation said, "Thanks be to God."

"Let the word of Christ dwell in you richly" (Col. 3:16). This must refer to the Scripture reading. The fact that it is the word "of Christ" suggests that they already had collections of Christ's sayings or perhaps an early form of the Gospel account. Or Paul could be speaking of the Old Testament Scriptures, viewed in the light of Christ. Thus it would be the word "about Christ."

"As you teach and admonish one another with all wisdom" (Col. 3:16). There was a preaching ministry going on here, but it was not what we are used to. Apparently there was no single preacher explaining Scripture to the rest. Various church members shared their knowledge, with perhaps some elders assuring that there was "wisdom" involved, too. (Remember the "message of wisdom" from 1 Cor. 12.)

"And as you sing psalms, hymns and spiritual songs with gratitude in your hearts to God" (Col. 3:16). Finally we get to the singing. The Passover service ended with singing, so the disciples at the end of the Last Supper sang a hymn and "went out to the Mount of Olives" (Matt. 26:30). The church incorporated this pattern into its services. After the preaching and teaching, they would sing.

Paul concluded with a well-known verse. We usually apply this to our daily lives, and that is fine. But I'm suggesting that his original intent had to do with the corporate worship service. "And whatever you do, whether in word or deed, do it all in the name of the Lord Jesus, giving thanks to God the Father through him."

Remember what we have said about energy and form. Paul was not stipulating forms here. He was not telling the Colossians to baptize a certain way or say the Lord's Prayer or pass the peace. He was observing their service and pressing them deeper into the Spirit's energy.

The Colossians seemed to have a pretty healthy church, except for one problem. They were beset by legalists. Certain teachers were saying, "Do not handle! Do not taste! Do not touch!" (Col. 2:21). We don't know if these were Orthodox Jews or ascetic Greeks, but they were having an effect on the Colossian church. These rules were "based on human commands and teachings," Paul wrote. "Such regulations indeed have an appearance of wisdom, with their self-imposed worship [the Greek word, a strange one, means 'the rigid control of one's desires'], their false humility and their harsh treatment of the body, but they lack any value in restraining sensual indulgence" (Col. 2:22-23).

Game-playing. That was the danger the Colossians faced. Maybe you have done this, too. You go to church and put on a show. You feel lousy; you want to be home in bed. But you go to church and do everything right, observe the forms, sing the hymns, say hello to the right people. You get home and you realize, "I never thought about God that whole time." On the surface you were a model worshiper, but you were just playing the game.

And that is the danger of legalism. It looks good, but it has no spiritual energy. Under the surface it is dead.

So Paul urged the Colossians to breathe life beneath the surface. Fill those forms with inner meaning. Don't just pray for forgiveness; forgive. Don't just pass the peace; let it control your heart. Don't just hear the Scripture, let it live within you. Don't just sing the songs; let them express your deep gratitude to God.

And whatever you do, in word or deed, don't just play games; do it in Jesus' name.

ELEVEN
THE BOOK OF
REVELATION
EXPLAINED

"What do you want to study?"

A dozen teenagers sat in front of me. I was leading their youth group in a Bible study. We had been going through 1 Peter and their interest had petered out. So I figured I would give them a chance to choose.

"Anything," I promised. "Whatever book of the Bible you want, we'll do. Anything at all."

Their answer was unanimous.

"Revelation!"

I gulped. "Anything except Revelation, that is."

These kids had seen movies like *Thief in the Night* with chilling tales of the end times. Some had seen quasi-religious movies like *The Omen* and were adding up everyone's name to total 666. To them, Revelation was a toy chest of weird symbols and spine tingles—a cross between *Friday the Thirteenth* and *Star Wars*. It scared their socks off. And they loved it.

Revelation scared me, too, but for different reasons. I didn't know what all those symbols meant, and I knew they would ask me. I knew I would end up dividing the 144,000 by the seventy weeks and get only twenty-three elders or something. And then some "pre-trib" parent would accuse me of teaching "post-trib" theology, when the truth was I just couldn't handle the higher math.

We never did study Revelation, and now I'm sorry because somewhere along the line I learned that Revelation is a book of worship. Its signs and symbols can titillate those so inclined, but the center of this vision—its main point—is the praise continually offered up to God by the saints and angels.

We must be careful as we approach the worship mentioned in Revelation. John was not telling people how to worship. But he was presenting a picture of ideal, eternal worship. Our situations are, of course, very different. We have tenors in the choir who can't sing. We have twenty minutes of announcements to give. We have watches that beep at twelve noon. The beasts and elders of Revelation don't have to deal with all that.

But Revelation can acquaint us with the essence of worship. It can give us a picture of where we are headed. And it should certainly remind us that what we do on Sunday mornings is no blip on the radar screen of human history, no exception to the rule, no passing fancy. It is what we will be doing forever. So we had better get used to it.

After recording the Lord's critiques of the seven churches of Asia Minor, John opened the curtain on his heavenly vision. Four living creatures with wings and lots of eyes are surrounding God's throne singing: "Holy, holy, holy is the Lord God Almighty, who was, and is, and is to come" (Rev. 4:8).

Don't you have a feeling of deja vu? Haven't we seen this somewhere before?

Yes, at the start of Isaiah's ministry, he saw a similar vision. Six-winged angels were flying around the throne singing, "Holy, holy, holy is the Lord Almighty, the whole earth is full of his glory" (Isa. 6:3). How did Isaiah respond? He became deeply aware of his own sin. Confronted by the awesome holiness of God, Isaiah realized how impure he was.

The response in Revelation is similar:

> Whenever the living creatures give glory, honor and thanks to him who sits on the throne and who lives for ever and ever, the twenty-four elders fall down before him who sits on the throne, and worship him who lives for ever and ever. They lay their crowns before the throne and say: "You are worthy, our Lord and God, to receive glory and honor and power, for you created all things, and by your will they were created and have their being." (Rev. 4:9-11)

It was not John who responded in humility. He was just watching this drama. It was the twenty-four elders who bowed down in worship before the Lord. In the strange numerology of this book, it is a pretty safe bet that the twenty-four elders represent the twelve tribes of Israel plus the twelve apostles of Christ. Old Testament and New Testament join together in acknowledging God's greatness. You might even imagine Isaiah as one of those twenty-four, casting their crowns before God's throne.

Already we have one major theme of the worship in this book: holiness. The triple utterance of the adjective certainly intensifies it: God is very, very holy. It may also be a hint of the Trinity: every aspect of God's personhood is holy. In Scripture, holiness carries the idea of being set apart, special. God is beyond us. Like Isaiah, we cringe at our own lack of holiness.

God is also called Almighty. The Greek word is *pantokrator.* We have bureaucrats who rule over bureaus, and autocrats who rule by themselves, and Democrats who believe in the rule of the people. We might call God a "Pantocrat." He rules over everything. Here is a second theme of Revelation. There may be wars and revolutions and plagues and people putting numbers on your forehead—but God is ultimately in charge. He will win out.

The creatures also say that the Lord "was and is and is to come." John has already used this catchy phrase twice in his first chapter (1:4, 8). It harks back to the way God introduced himself to Moses at the burning bush (Exod. 3). "I am 'I AM,'" the Lord said. That is essentially what "Yahweh" means: I AM. The Lord is existence, he is being. And his being transcends time.

Jesus answered a tough question by referring to God's introduction to Moses. The Sadducees, who did not believe in any afterlife, had asked a hypothetical stumper. It was about the "resurrection"—life in heaven. They were trying to show how absurd the whole notion was. But Jesus quoted from the burning-bush story. God had said, "I am the God of Abraham, Isaac, and Jacob." Now, if those patriarchs were dead and gone, he would have said, "*I was . . .*" Therefore, since he was still their God, Abraham, Isaac, and Jacob still had to be living somewhere. Because they worshiped him as God, their existence continues.

This would have been very important for John's readers to remember. He was probably writing in the nineties, during the reign of the

Roman emperor Domitian, who was persecuting the church. Times were tough. There would be no doubt about God's great acts of the past. Certainly, he *was*.

But John's readers needed assurance that he hadn't left them. They needed to feel his presence in the present moment. They needed a God who *is*.

And yet there might be concerns about where all this was leading. Even if God was with them at the moment, the future looked bleak. Would the worship of God continue, or would the Romans snuff it out? God assures them that he is to come. The future belongs to him as well.

Note that the elders cast their crowns before the throne. This was what a defeated king would do before a victorious king. It was a sign of submission. It is what Herod should have done before the Christ-child.

Where did they get these crowns? From God, no doubt. We have a picture of God's kingdom in which they—and we—are subrulers, kings and priests. But all that authority must be laid before God's feet.

The elders say, "You are worthy, our Lord and God, to receive glory and honor and power." *Worthy* is a comparative concept. Someone is worthy of something or worthy to do something. "The worker is worth his keep," Jesus said (Matt. 10:10). John the Baptist said he was not worthy to untie Jesus' shoes (John 1:27). The repentant Prodigal Son told his father, "I am no longer worthy to be called your son" (Luke 15:21). The idea is "good enough."

Isn't that a strange way to refer to God? "You're good enough to receive my worship." That is a supreme understatement. We just saw Isaiah shrinking before God's holiness, considering himself unworthy even to speak in the Lord's presence. Now the elders tell God he is "good enough"?

First, let us see what he is "good enough" for. Glory, honor, power. That is pretty high-level acclaim. Second, consider that he is the only one who is worthy of all this. And third, note an additional nuance to this "worthy" concept. Paul wrote to the Thessalonians, "We ought always to thank God for you, brothers, and rightly so" (2 Thess. 1:3). "Rightly so" is literally "as it is worthy [or proper]." The same Greek word is used. For Paul, it was right to thank God because their faith was growing, all sorts of good things were happening. For the elders, it is right to give God glory, honor, and power.

So what starts out as an understatement becomes a piece of great praise. We have a desire to worship, a need to worship, but no one is good enough to worship—except God, the Creator of all things. Because he is the Creator, he deserves our praise. All things—including us—exist because he wants them to. Thus it is proper for us to glorify him. His will is the driving force behind all that is. And so he is worthy of all we can give him, all that we are.

There is another significant phrase here. The elders direct their praises to the "Lord and God." This would have rung bells with John's readers, as the Roman emperor, Domitian, was at that time demanding that everyone worship him. It was a show of patriotism. One signaled his loyalty to Rome by praising the emperor. He wanted to be called "Lord and God" (*dominus et deus*).

Christians, of course, couldn't cooperate. They wanted to be good citizens, but Jesus was their only Lord. To pray in this way to the emperor would be idolatry. And so they were persecuted, hunted down and killed in gruesome ways.

Domitian was not worthy of glory, honor, and power. Only the true "Lord and God" was. By acknowledging the Lord as the only one worthy of worship, the elders were declaring their allegiance, showing which side they were on.

The story is told of a deaf mute who faithfully attended church each Sunday. Finally, someone asked him, "Why do you keep coming when you can't hear what's being said?" In response, he wrote, "I come each week to let people know which side I am on."[1] He had the right idea. Each week many other pursuits vie for our attention—and for our worship. Money, success, relationships, pleasure. These want to be "Lord and God" in our lives. But God deserves our presence in Christian worship (as well as our obedience day by day). We declare our allegiance by being there.

Note some of the key points about worship we have seen:

1. Worship encounters God's utter holiness.

2. Worship acknowledges God's great power.

3. Worship celebrates the everlastingness of God. We praise him for past acts, exult in his presence, and commit to him our future.

4. A proper response to all of the above is to bow in humility and submission.

5. Worshiping God is the right thing to do, the most appropriate thing that we will ever do. He created us and sustains us by his will. He made us to be worshipers and empowers us to worship him.

6. He is the supreme Lord and God, as no one else is. Worship is a way to show whose side we are on.

In Revelation 5 we meet the Lamb. This is obviously Jesus, who was the sacrificial offering for our sins. The creatures and elders fall before the Lamb.

> And they sang a new song: "You are worthy to take the scroll and to open its seals, because you were slain, and with your blood you purchased men for God from every tribe and language and people and nation. You have made them to be a kingdom and priests to serve our God, and they will reign on the earth." Then I looked and heard the voice of many angels, numbering thousands upon thousands, and ten thousand times ten thousand. They encircled the throne and the living creatures and the elders. In a loud voice they sang: "Worthy is the Lamb, who was slain, to receive power and wealth and wisdom and strength and honor and glory and praise!" Then I heard every creature in heaven and on earth and under the earth and on the sea, and all that is in them, singing: "To him who sits on the throne and to the Lamb be praise and honor and glory and power, for ever and ever!" The four living creatures said, "Amen," and the elders fell down and worshiped. (Rev. 5:9-14)

It starts with a "new song." The word for "new" does not just mean "recent" (that would be *neos* in the Greek). This is *kainos;* it means a whole new kind of thing. William Barclay wrote, "*Kainos* describes a thing which has not only been recently produced; it describes a thing the like of which has never existed before."[2] The psalmist often implored his people, "Sing to the LORD a new song" (Pss. 33:3; 40:3; 98:1; 144:9; 149:1). But this new song may be more along the lines of Isaiah's prophecy.

"Sing to the LORD a new song," the prophet wrote, "his praise from the ends of the earth. . . . The LORD will march out like a mighty man, like a warrior he will stir up his zeal; with a shout he will raise the battle cry and will triumph over his enemies" (Isa. 42:10, 13).

What's so new about this song?

First, we find ourselves with a *new situation*. It is the end of history. The scroll of the future is held in the Lord's hand—he is about to break its seals. The song of the Lord's triumph—and of his ultimate worth—is appropriate in any new situation in which we find ourselves.

Second, there is a *new recipient* of the song. The first "worthy" song of Revelation (4:11) was sung to the Creator. Because of his creation, he was worthy of our praise. Like generations of Old Testament believers, the elders glorified God the Father for his creative control of the universe.

But here in chapter 5, the pages of the New Testament crack open. The multitude sings, "Worthy is the Lamb, who was slain." The Second Person of the Godhead is offered power and wealth and wisdom and strength and honor and glory and praise. It is not a show of power now that wins him glory, but a show of love. He was killed. With his blood he redeemed us—Gentiles as well as Jews.

Third, he is doing a *new thing*. Even back in Isaiah 42, the Lord was talking about this: "New things I declare; before they spring into being I announce them to you" (Isa. 42:9). He went on to announce the Lord's ultimate triumph over evil.

Revelation picks up the story of this new thing God is doing through Christ. God has taken people from all over the earth, and, "You have made them to be a kingdom and priests to serve our God, and they will reign on the earth."

That is us, folks. A kingdom and priests. Notice he did not say we are kings; that might deflect from Christ's ultimate authority. Together, under his authority, we are a kingdom. We will have the kind of authority over the earth that God created us to have (Gen. 1:26).

And we are priests. Old Testament priests were set apart, special. They had access to God that the common people did not have. But now we all have access to God through Christ. This is the essence of the new song we sing.

After the new song is sung, the creatures say, "Amen." Nothing else need be said. There is a time to say new things and there is a time to affirm what has already been said.

Worship should be full of new songs. God's mercies are new every morning (Lam. 3:23), and our appreciation of them should reflect that newness. Our minds and hearts should eagerly seek new, wonderful ways to praise our great God.

But sometimes we need to stop and affirm what a previous generation has done or said. We need to say amen to the truths that have been learned before.

Pause again for some more tidbits of worship from Revelation 5.

7. Christian worship can be characterized as a "new song."

97

8. The church finds itself in new situations as time goes on. Christian worship can relate to new circumstances.

9. We worship not only God the Creator but also Jesus the Savior.

10. Jesus is worthy of worship because he was slain. His sacrifice for our sin should be central to our worship.

11. Christian worship should acknowledge the new things God is doing in us and for us—our relationship to God as well as our interactions with this earth.

12. There is a time for new songs, and there is a time to say amen.

Fast-forward to Revelation 19. We are skipping lots of wars and disasters, but we reach one phenomenal worship service in this chapter.

> After this I heard what sounded like the roar of a great multitude in heaven shouting: "Hallelujah! Salvation and glory and power belong to our God, for true and just are his judgments. He has condemned the great prostitute who corrupted the earth by her adulteries. He has avenged on her the blood of his servants." And again they shouted: "Hallelujah! The smoke from her goes up for ever and ever." The twenty-four elders and the four living creatures fell down and worshiped God, who was seated on the throne. And they cried: "Amen, Hallelujah!" Then a voice came from the throne, saying: "Praise our God, all you his servants, you who fear him, both small and great!"
>
> Then I heard what sounded like a great multitude, like the roar of rushing waters and like loud peals of thunder, shouting: "Hallelujah! For our Lord God Almighty reigns. Let us rejoice and be glad and give him glory! For the wedding of the Lamb has come, and his bride has made herself ready. Fine linen, bright and clean, was given her to wear." (Fine linen stands for the righteous acts of the saints.) Then the angel said to me, "Write: 'Blessed are those who are invited to the wedding supper of the Lamb!'" And he added, "These are the true words of God." At this I fell at his feet to worship him. But he said to me, "Do not do it! I am a fellow servant with you and with your brothers who hold to the testimony of Jesus. Worship God! For the testimony of Jesus is the spirit of prophecy." (Rev. 19:1-11)

"Hallelujah!" it begins. You know this word. It means simply, "Praise God!" The word is Hebrew. The rest of this book is, of course,

Greek. It is as if I suddenly mentioned John's *modus operandi*. As you see, I just slid into Latin. I could have said, "way of operating," but for some reason I felt the Latin phrase communicated better what I wanted to say (or impressed you more).

So why did John use a Hebrew phrase here? This is the only place in the New Testament where *Hallelujah* appears, but it is all over the Psalms. And it must have played a crucial role in Israel's worship. In fact, in one section (Pss. 111–117) nearly every psalm begins or ends with Hallelujah. Psalm 135 begins:

> *Hallelujah!* Praise [*Hallelu*] the name of the LORD; praise [*hallelu*] him, you servants of the LORD, you who minister in the house of the LORD, in the courts of the house of our God. Hallelujah! For the LORD is good. (Ps. 135:1-3, NIV adjusted to reflect Hebrew)

The word would certainly have called to mind the worship that took place in the Jerusalem temple. John and other Jewish believers would have remembered the temple worship as a glorious experience that was somehow missing something—missing the fulfillment of Christ. By John's time, the church may have incorporated the saying of Hallelujah into its own service. And John's vision indicates that, even though the temple itself was now destroyed, the glory of its worship continued in heaven and would continue through eternity, directed toward both the Creator and the Lamb. As the psalmist wrote: "Let this be written for a future generation, that a people not yet created may praise the LORD [Hallelujah]" (Ps. 102:18).

The final page of history is about to be turned, and the worshiping multitude returns to the simple praise of the psalmist. "Praise to Yahweh!"

"Salvation and glory and power belong to our God!" In a way, this is a postlude to the triumphal entry. There, Jesus had ridden into Jerusalem amid shouts of "Hosanna!" As we have seen, this was a word of praise, but it also was a cry for deliverance. Literally it means, "Lord, save us!" Here at the end of history, the Lord has saved us. He answers our praising Hosanna with his mighty salvation—and we respond with Hallelujah.

You might say that all our worship fits between Hosanna and Hallelujah. "You are great because you can save us" leads to "You are great because you have saved us."

Picture it happening in your church. The great multitude rises to sing a Hallelujah chorus. "Salvation, glory, and power," they thunder, and our hearts rise with their sounds. They sing the mighty refrain— "True and just are his judgments"—and we thrill with the power of their vocal attack. They swing into the next verse, singing, "He has condemned the great prostitute. . . ."

Wait a second. We look down nervously as they trill about her "adul-ul-ul-ulteries."

We don't hear many great anthems about prostitutes and their adulteries—and with good reason. But here in the greatest anthem of history, the singers do not shy away from the grim realities of life. The Lord is great because he confronted the sin of his enemies and judged them for it. True and just are his judgments.

The song turns downright mean. "He has avenged on her the blood of his servants. . . . The smoke from her goes up for ever and ever." This calls to mind some of David's vindictive psalms: "Crush my enemies, Lord."

The same questions you have always asked about those vindictive psalms apply here. What is this vengeful spirit doing in a hymn of praise?

First, we are dealing with ultimate evil. The "prostitute" has violently opposed God and his people. Earlier the prostitute is called "Babylon," which served as a code name for Rome. John's readers were suffering a vicious persecution under emperor Domitian. Undoubtedly, they cried out for God's intervention. Through John, God promises that ultimately he will intervene. At the end of history he will judge those who have opposed him and hurt his people.

Second, remember that the Christian principle of nonretribution is based on the idea that "it is mine to avenge; I will repay, says the LORD" (Rom. 12:19; Deut. 32:35). We are to "love our enemies" (Matt. 5:44) because God loves them enough to offer them a chance to repent. But at the end of time, when they still haven't repented, the Lord wreaks his vengeance. We can praise him for that.

That gives us another clue about our own worship. It does not have to ignore evil. In light of God's holiness, we can announce his judgment on the evil of our society. Our worship should have that prophetic edge.

Two cautions, however. Remember that our first response to God's holiness should be a consciousness of our own sin. And remember that

God does love even the evil people of this world. We must reflect that love even as we condemn their sin.

The worship continues with a call to God's servants (*douloi*, slaves) to praise him. Also invited are "you who fear him, both small and great." It's a minor point, but let me suggest that these are two different groups of people (the Greek throws in the word *kai*, so it would read either "and you who fear him" or "even you who fear him"). Fear is one appropriate emotion of worship, but I think the bondslaves (*douloi*) have gone beyond that—into commitment. The bondslave was a temporary servant who decided to commit himself to his master for life, usually out of some sort of devotion or sense of security. In the New Testament the word applies to Christians.

But the fearers are merely responding to the moment. God has scored a stunning victory and they are scared to death. I am not saying that these "outsiders" share in all the benefits of the banquet, but Scripture does indicate that everyone will ultimately have to recognize the power of God and the lordship of Christ (Phil. 2:10-11—"every knee should bow . . . and every tongue confess that Jesus Christ is Lord, to the glory of God the Father").

"Both small and great" bow in respect before the victorious Lord. Fear is a great leveler. I am writing this in the days after an earthquake rocked San Francisco. The news reports have shown baseball players and groundskeepers, councilmen and cab drivers, executives and sec- retaries—all shuddering with fear over what might have happened. Next to God's power, there is no small or great. Human distinctions disappear.

We should remember that in our own worship. I keep trying to sing better than everyone around me. God humbled me once by seating me next to a man in my church who could not carry a tune—but sang as loud as he could. I struggled to stay on key, silently irked at this man's voice. He was throwing me off, making me sound bad. I hoped that people would not look back and think that I was responsible for those awful sounds. Surely they knew I sang better than that. And then I thought, *Who is really worshiping here?* It wasn't I.

When we fully realize God's greatness, concerns for our own status become trivial, inappropriate.

Fear turns to joy. We've seen this before (see chapter 3). Naturally, we fear God's holy power. But that fear becomes joy when I realize that his power is on my side.

101

There is one Christian leader I used to fear. He invited me to breakfast to discuss a writing project, and I shuddered inside as I ate my bacon. He was famous, important. I was just a year out of college. What if he didn't like me?

But he did, I guess. The project worked well. And there were other breakfasts. At some point I realized that he was inviting me to breakfast just because he wanted to talk, to keep up with me, not for any particular project. He was my friend. Suddenly the fear vanished. In its place was joy. All that "importance" that once kept me at a distance was now "on my side," working to my advantage. He could give me more projects to do, he could recommend me to others. I enjoyed that, but most of all I enjoyed him. We were now free to enjoy each other's friendship.

Similarly, the Lord invites us to share a meal with him—the marriage feast of the Lamb. The fear that had kept us on our knees turns to joy. He helps us up and seats us at his banquet table. We are free to enjoy the Lord's friendship. But we suddenly find that we are not only friends, but the bride herself. Together, as the church, we can share the most intimate of relationships with our Savior.

But wait! What happened to "Holy, holy, holy"? What about the awesome greatness of God? What about our humble kneeling before him, our recognition of our own sin? Certainly we are not worthy to even attend this wedding banquet, much less walk down the aisle. We are like the poor man in Jesus' parable who showed up at a wedding without the proper garments and had to be thrown out (Matt. 22:11-13). We try to be good enough, but as Isaiah wrote, "All our righteous acts are like filthy rags" (Isa. 64:6). We're like spiritual Cinderellas, longing to go to the great feast, but we have nothing to wear.

Fine linen.

The Lord himself invites us. The Lord himself will clothe us.

Fine linen, bright and clean.

The Lord dresses us in his perfection. We are radiant with his glory.

"Fine linen, bright and clean, was given her to wear. (Fine linen stands for the righteous acts of the saints.)"

What righteous acts? I thought our "righteous acts" were filthy rags. Is this saying that the saints have earned their bright robes by doing good deeds? No. Notice that the linen "was given" to the saints. This is entirely God's doing.

The Epistle to the Romans may explain it. The word for "righteous acts" (*dikaiomata*) is used five times, and translated five different ways by the NIV. As you will see, there is a single idea here, but it changes slightly with its context.

In Romans 1:32, Paul spoke of "God's righteous decree" that those who commit the horrible sins he has just mentioned deserve death. A "righteous act" in this case is a decree by which God demands righteousness and punishes sin.

In Romans 2:26, Paul spoke of Gentiles who keep "the law's requirements," the same word. Now "righteous acts" are those deeds that God requires in order to declare someone righteous. Of course, the next chapter breaks the news that no one can fully satisfy God's requirements.

In Romans 5:16, Paul spoke of the gift of God's grace that brought "justification" for many sins. The "righteous act" is a decree again, but not a decree of judgment or demand. This decree declares that someone is righteous—even though he has sinned.

In Romans 5:18, Paul compared how Adam's one sin brought condemnation to all humanity with how Jesus' one "act of righteousness" brought justification and life. Here it is the act by which God declares his people righteous. That act is, of course, Jesus' sacrificial death.

In Romans 8:4, Paul spoke of Christ's death as a sin offering, condemning sin, so that "the righteous requirements of the law" might be fully met in the lives of believers. Here again, the "righteous acts" are what the Lord requires in order to declare us righteous.

All of this makes it very difficult to translate the "fine linen" of Revelation 19. We might say, "Fine linen stands for the righteous act of Jesus' death, which has satisfied God's demands for righteousness for each one of them."

People come to worship in their Sunday best. Their clothes are pressed and tailored. Their faces are made up, their hair in place. But sometimes I think they also press their souls.

You know what I mean. People pretend to be holy when they are not. They put on a mask of righteousness when their insides are filthy rags.

People *should* prepare for worship. They should get things right with God. But we must always remember that it is God who clothes us to come into his presence. I do not impress him with my fancy tie or my three-piece attitude. He gives me his fine linen to wear. That means I can be honest about who I am, where I'm coming from.

103

The "wedding supper" of the Lamb gives us a nice picture of worship. Maybe we should think of our worship services as wedding receptions. There is joy and fellowship—but the whole occasion is directed toward the bride and groom. We celebrate the relationship between Christ and his church.

John was so overwhelmed by the scene that he fell down to worship the angel who served as guide for this heavenly tour. The angel stopped him. God alone deserves worship.

This would have struck deeply at any Gnostics who might have been reading this. The Gnostics had been spreading their heresy in the church in various forms, and would continue to plague Christianity. They claimed to have secret knowledge of God, which they received through angels. In fact, many of them saw Christ as one of these angelic mediators along the ladder to God. Some developed elaborate systems of angel-worship.

John has an angel showing him through this vision, but he stops short of worshiping him. At the center of this whole book is Jesus. Nothing should detract from the worship of Jesus Christ.

There is an ancient story of a king who got bad news and killed the messenger. In our churches we sometimes do the opposite, but it is just as silly. We get Good News and we worship the messenger. Billy Graham, Chuck Swindoll, Tony Campolo, our own pastors—surely they would say to us, "Do not do it! I am a fellow servant with you and with your brothers who hold to the testimony of Jesus! Worship God!"

The angel adds a curious phrase: "The testimony of Jesus is the spirit of prophecy." Donald Grey Barnhouse commented, "The possession of the prophetic spirit will always manifest itself in a witness to Jesus. The angel has been the bearer of a wonderful prophecy which John has recognized as divine and which has brought him to the point of worship. . . . When the worship has been attempted by John and rejected by the angel, the latter explains that worship of the Lord Jesus Christ is the mark of the prophetic spirit and the two must go together. Thus, in a simple sentence, the Book does away with all false prophets whose main object is always to draw men away from the witness of Christ."[3]

The challenge applies to our worship services today. If they are to be truly filled with the prophetic spirit of God's truth, they will be witnesses to Jesus.

He alone is worthy of our worship.

Let us sum up our worship ideas from Revelation 19.

13. We praise God in worship with "Hallelujah!"—thanking him for the salvation he has provided.

14. Worship may have to confront the evil of the world around us, proclaiming God's judgment on human wickedness (but we should maintain humility and love).

15. In worship, our fear turns to joy.

16. God himself provides the righteousness we need to come before him in worship. We can thus be honest with ourselves, each other, and God as we approach him.

17. Worship is, in a way, a wedding reception, celebrating a loving, committed relationship.

18. We must worship God alone, not those who serve him.

Notes

1. Daniel D. Walker, *Enemy in the Pew?* (New York, Harper & Row, 1967), 60, quoted in Robert W. Bailey, *New Ways in Christian Worship* (Nashville: Broadman, 1981), 23).
2. William Barclay, *The Revelation of St. John,* vol. 1 (Philadelphia: Westminster Press, 1959), 223.
3. Donald Gray Barnhouse, *Revelation: An Expository Commentary* (Grand Rapids: Zondervan, 1971), 354.

TWELVE
FIRST THINGS
FIRST
(OLD TESTAMENT LAW)

Just imagine that a new president is taking office and wants to appoint a panel that would be representative of the entire nation. The president is troubled. Who gets named to this panel? Well, the president's first instinct might be to name his friends, people he trusts: cabinet members, senators, old school chums. But these would just tell him what he already knows. He needs a more balanced view.

So he finds several women for this committee, a few blacks, an Oriental, a native American. He finds some elderly people, a recent college grad, and a teenager. He names a homeless person and a disabled person. In each case he tries not to compromise quality. He chooses the most thoughtful, observant people he can.

The press decries all this as tokenism. And it would be if he were doing it all for show. But, in our fictional account here, let us give the president the benefit of the doubt. Let's say he truly wants to see the nation through these people's eyes.

Later the nation begins to pull together. The elderly complain less because they know that someone who understands them has the president's ear. The native Americans gain some confidence because one of their own is advising the head of state. Racial tension eases in the cities of the nation. The diverse groups within the country pull together because these leading members of those groups have pulled together. Because these individuals are honored by the president, all of these groups feel honored.

This is a fantasy and certainly a bit naive. But it illustrates a crucial Old Testament principle of worship: the concept of firstfruits. The part sanctifies the whole.

We get our first taste of it in Exodus: "Celebrate the Feast of Harvest with the firstfruits of the crops you sow in your field. . . . Bring the best of the firstfruits of your soil to the house of the LORD your God" (23:16, 19).

The "firstfruits" were naturally the first crops to grow in each new harvest season. These belonged to the Lord. The concept is even broader a few chapters later: "The first offspring of every womb belongs to me, including all the firstborn males of your livestock, whether from herd or flock. . . . Redeem all your firstborn sons" (Exod. 34:19-20).

Firstborn animals would be sacrificed to the Lord. A firstborn son was redeemed by parents making a special animal sacrifice. The principle is remarkable—the first child belongs to God. Parents can raise him as their own, but they must "buy him back" first.

Each year there was a special feast of firstfruits, immediately following Passover, as the spring's early harvest was coming up. (The timing of this feast may have varied, depending on the climate, and different farmers may have brought their firstfruits to the temple at different times.)

Leviticus marks out the ritual involved:

> When you enter the land I am going to give you and you reap its harvest, bring to the priest a sheaf of the first grain you harvest. He is to wave the sheaf before the LORD so it will be accepted on your behalf. . . . You must not eat any bread, or roasted or new grain, until the very day you bring this offering to your God. (Lev. 23:10-14)

Imagine: You have gone all winter on food from the barn, stored up from last year's harvest. It is getting stale. It may be running out. You have planted the early crops and have waited patiently as they grew. Finally, harvesttime arrives. You go out in your fields and bring back bushels of grain. It looks so good—fresh and healthy.

But you can't eat it.

"You must not eat it," the law says. That first portion belongs to God. You must take it to the temple, where a priest waves a sheaf before the Lord. That simple act says, "This is yours, Lord." Then that grain is eaten by the priests and Levites, who have no land of their own to farm. You return to your farm—probably very hungry—to partake of the rest of that early harvest.

Why? What is the sense of this offering? Deuteronomy gives us some insight:

> When you have entered the land the LORD your God is giving you as an inheritance and have taken possession of it and settled in it, take some of the firstfruits of all that you produce from the soil of the land the LORD your God is giving you and put them in a basket. Then go to a place the LORD your God will choose as a dwelling for his Name and say to the priest in office at the time, "I declare today to the LORD your God that I have come to the land the LORD swore to our forefathers to give us." The priest shall take the basket from your hands and set it down in front of the altar of the LORD your God. Then you shall declare before the LORD your God: "My father was a wandering Aramean, and he went down into Egypt with a few people and lived there and became a great nation, powerful and numerous. But the Egyptians mistreated us and made us suffer, putting us to hard labor. Then we cried out to the LORD, the God of our fathers, and the LORD heard our voice and saw our misery, toil and oppression. So the LORD brought us out of Egypt with a mighty hand and an outstretched arm, with great terror and with miraculous signs and wonders. He brought us to this place and gave us this land, a land flowing with milk and honey; and now I bring the firstfruits of the soil that you, O LORD, have given me." Place the basket before the LORD your God and bow down before him. And you and the Levites and the aliens among you shall rejoice in all the good things the LORD your God has given to you and your household. (Deut. 26:1-11)

In my church—and maybe in yours—the collection of the offering is preceded by the pastor's prayer. The ushers have lined up, plates in their hands, and are ready for action. Sometimes the pastor prays on and on: "Lord, thank you for lifting us up from the miry clay. . . ." Our entire salvation-history, Genesis to Revelation, gets covered in this precollection prayer. Not that I'm peeking or anything, but the ushers usually start flexing their knees, trying to keep their feet from going numb. The pastor finally says, "Amen," and they stagger down the aisle, regaining feeling with each step.

Now I realize that has biblical precedent. Here in Deuteronomy the giver is to recite this lengthy account of the history of Israel. Why? Because giving to God is never just a momentary act. It is based on the past.

Five times in eleven verses this passage explicitly notes that God was giving the land to the Israelites. That giving of the land was a lengthy process, taking hundreds of years, and at this writing they still hadn't taken possession of it. But God would be faithful to his word, even if he had to work miracles to get his people back in their land. Oops! No, it's not "their land." It is the land God promised to give them.

Therefore, the crops that the land produces are not "their crops." They are "the good things the LORD your God has given to you and your household." Those crops belong to God.

Conceivably, God could demand all of the produce. But he is a giver. He knows his people need to eat and trade to live. So he asks only the first part. This is the "sacred portion" (Deut. 26:13-14) to be given to him in a special way.

This offering of the sacred portion, the "firstfruits," does two things. (1) It recognizes God's true ownership of the land and what it produces. (2) It feeds God's special people. Some of the produce given would be burnt as a sacrifice, but much of it would be given to feed not only the priests and Levites, but also widows, orphans, and immigrants from other lands.

In Ezekiel, the "firstfruits" idea is extended to the land itself. The prophet saw a vision in which a future Israel is divided up by the various tribes. But in the center, he said, is a "sacred portion," to be given to the priests and Levites. "This is the best of the land and must not pass into other hands, because it is holy to the LORD" (Ezek. 48:14).

Notice that this is the "best" of the land. This adds to the firstfruits concept. It is not only the first portion that God wants but the best. Numbers 18:12 speaks of the "finest olive oil and all the finest new wine and grain they give the LORD as the firstfruits of their harvest." Perhaps we are talking about the portion we are the most reluctant to give up. Yet that is exactly the portion God requires.

It makes sense that the Levites get the firstfruits of land and crops because they are the "firstfruits" of God's people. Remember how the

Israelites had to "redeem" their firstborn sons? The Levites took their place.

The Lord also said to Moses, "I have taken the Levites from among the Israelites in place of the first male offspring of every Israelite woman. The Levites are mine, for all the firstborn are mine" (Num. 3:11-13).

Does this mean that the other Israelites did not belong to the Lord? No. The Levites belonged to him in a special way. If you are a non-Levite, should you feel left out because of this? No. The whole nation "belongs to God" even more because this special group is specially dedicated.

The Apostle Paul described the way this worked in ancient Israel: "If the part of the dough offered as firstfruits is holy, then the whole batch is holy" (Rom. 11:16). You harvest the grain, grind it to make flour, form that into dough, and bake bread. Then you take the first loaf and set it apart to God. You give it to the priests or the poor or whatever—but that belongs to God in a special way (Num. 15:17-21). But because you have done that, the rest of the dough is holy. You may eat it in health, and that will please God, because you have recognized him as the giver of the whole batch. The special offering of the part sanctifies the whole.

This truth has many powerful implications for Christian worship. We will cover these more thoroughly in a later chapter. But it is clear that we owe God our best—not only of the money we give, but of the worship we offer. The best music, the best movement, the best listening, the best speaking.

This presents a strong argument for the importance of corporate worship services. Many say, "I worship God with my whole life. I don't need to go to church on Sunday." They're missing the point. The Sunday service is not a gift given in place of the rest of the week. It is our firstfruits offering. We give him Sunday morning in a special way as we recognize his ownership of every part of our lives. The part sanctifies the whole. We still have responsibility to live Monday-to-Saturday according to God's desires, but God allows us to go about our business. We can adopt a pray-without-ceasing attitude, in constant communication with God, but we don't have to spend all our waking hours on our knees. We can drive and shop and talk on the phone and drive hard business deals, relaxing in God's ownership of our lives. We know and he knows that we belong to him; we established that in church last Sunday.

111

But have you ever missed a Sunday? I have. And does this ever happen to you? You get to about Wednesday or Thursday and you're tired, or harried, or worried. It is as if you are running out of spiritual gas—except I've never wanted to think of church as a spiritual filling station. There is more to it.

I think it is like our telephones. Things used to be so easy before the AT&T breakup. AT&T owned our phones. We paid them a monthly rent for our phones. They took care of all the problems. For you and me, it was rather worry-free. More expensive, maybe, but no hassle.

Then everything changed. We were suddenly given the privilege of buying our own phones and phone service. Many of us bought cheap things on sale and plugged them in—only to be tormented by bad signals and frequent breakdowns. And, of course, the phone company says, "Sorry. It's not our phone—not our problem." But I didn't buy a cheap phone. I continue to rent my phone. I'm probably paying a lot more than I need to, but I don't have to worry about it. It's their phone.

Going to church is like paying your phone bill. We are "renting" our lives, paying God the weekly firstfruits of our worship. In this way we remind ourselves and God that he owns us.

But when we skip church, it is our way of buying our own cheap phone. Without that reminder that he owns us, we begin to think we can run our own lives. And maybe we can—for a few days. But then the worries start to pile up. Things go wrong. The phone breaks. We feel spiritually dry because we lack the spiritual resources to deal with our daily crises. When we get back to church, we show once again to ourselves and everyone else that we are only renters.

The Old Testament promises that things will go well for those who offer God their firstfruits. "Honor the LORD with your wealth, with the firstfruits of all your crops; then your barns will be filled to overflowing, and your vats will brim with new wine" (Prov. 3:9). We really can't handle the pressures of running our own lives. As we acknowledge God's ownership of us and all we have, we can relax in his ultimate control.

THIRTEEN
WHEN BAD THINGS HAPPEN TO GOOD WORSHIP
(OLD TESTAMENT PROPHETS)

Tokenism is always a problem. I may give a friend a gift as a "token of appreciation." But then she feels she has to give me a gift in return. That may not be a token of appreciation but of obligation. In some cities, lawyers give Christmas gifts to judges, not out of friendship, but out of a fear that they will lose cases if they don't. At some point, "tokens of appreciation" become bribes.

It happens with worship as well. We may start doing certain actions because they express our love for God. Say, raising our hands in the air. All of a sudden, one Sunday the Lord fills me with joy and I throw my arms upward in praise. So far, so good.

The next week I try it again. It feels good.

The next week I don't feel like worshiping. I don't know, I went to a party the night before and didn't get much sleep. I'm just not into it. But, raising my hands made me feel good last week, I'll try it again. And it works.

Time goes on and, for some reason, I'm losing touch with God. I'm going to more parties Saturday nights, and going to church bleary-eyed. Still, I raise my hands and usually I can get into the feeling of worship. But even that feeling begins to fade. The action doesn't work like it used to.

So this Sunday I show up and I really don't want to be there. I'm just going through the motions. And I just don't feel like raising my hands. But I look around and see everyone else in the church doing so.

If I don't, they'll think something is wrong between me and God. Which there is, but I can take care of it. So I raise my hands again—this time not in worship, not out of a desire to please God, not even in a desire to enjoy worship myself—just to look like I'm worshiping. The forms of worship have taken over. They now have no relationship with my spirit. They do not express what is really in my heart.

This is the kind of "dead," form-only worship Jesus opposed in John 4. The Old Testament prophets also opposed it—using some of the Bible's strongest language.

In his first chapter, Isaiah begins a tirade against the nation of Judah:

> Hear the word of the LORD, you rulers of Sodom; listen to the law of our God, you people of Gomorrah! "The multitude of your sacrifices—what are they to me?" says the LORD. "I have more than enough of burnt offerings, of rams and the fat of fattened animals; I have no pleasure in the blood of bulls and lambs and goats." (Isa. 1:10-11)

Isaiah began to prophesy during the reign of King Uzziah. In a lot of ways, King Uzziah was the Ronald Reagan of Judah. The nation was weak when Uzziah became king, and Uzziah made it strong. He scored a series of military victories. The tribute from the vanquished nations led to economic prosperity for Judah. Even spiritually, the country seemed to be doing well. Uzziah "did what was right in the eyes of the LORD" (2 Chron. 26:4). This indicates that Judah was not succumbing to idol-worship—a frequent problem in those days.

These verses in Isaiah indicate that the Jews were active in the worship of God. They brought a "multitude" of sacrifices to the temple. Burnt offerings, rams, bulls, goats, animals specially fattened for the sacrifice. They were apparently taking great care to make the sacrifices just right.

So what was the problem? Where does Isaiah get off calling them Sodom and Gomorrah?

Those were the cities of the Dead Sea plain that God destroyed with burning sulfur from heaven (Gen. 19). They were legendary for their sexual immorality. But their sin went beyond that. Isaiah himself said of his people: "They parade their sin like Sodom; they do not hide it" (Isa. 3:9). Apparently, it wasn't just their sin; it was their arrogant attitude about it.

114

Ezekiel confirmed this idea: "Now this was the sin of your sister Sodom: She and her daughters were arrogant, overfed and unconcerned; they did not help the poor and needy. They were haughty and did detestable things before me" (Ezek. 16:49-50). So we have a picture of a nation living in good times. The well-to-do enjoy their wealth. Living in luxury, they ignore the needs of the poor. Yet they feel no remorse. They continue to perform the religious rituals, confident that God is on their side. Peeking ahead to Isaiah 1:23, we get even more evidence of this life-style: "Your rulers are rebels, companions of thieves; they all love bribes and chase after gifts. They do not defend the cause of the fatherless; the widow's case does not come before them." The people most in need of justice are ignored by the judges, who take bribes from rich merchants and landlords.

Therefore, all the worship rituals were unacceptable to the Lord. "I have more than enough" means, "I am glutted." "I have no pleasure" in them anymore, he said.

The prophecy continued:

When you come to appear before me, who has asked this of you, this trampling of my courts? Stop bringing meaningless offerings! Your incense is detestable to me. New Moons, Sabbaths and convocations—I cannot bear your evil assemblies. Your New Moon festivals and your appointed feasts my soul hates. They have become a burden to me; I am weary of bearing them. (Isa. 1:12-14)

Trampling. That is all their worship was. They paraded in with their sacrificial animals and paraded out. Ezekiel used the same word to describe how strong sheep (symbolizing the rich) mess up the pasture for weak sheep (the poor). "Is it not enough for you to feed on the good pasture? Must you also trample the rest of the pasture with your feet?" (Ezek. 34:18). Perhaps the Lord was saying in Isaiah, "If you weren't always tramping through here with your meaningless offerings, then at least the poor could come in here and worship me."

Who invited you? That is what God seems to be asking. It could be taken two ways. First, note that the Jews seemed very interested in following the worship regulations to the letter. Here God announced through Isaiah: These meaningless offerings are not things I have required; they might work for Baal or someone else, but not me.

But, as the question is phrased, some arrogant worshiper might respond, "Why, you did, Lord. You have asked us—required us—to appear before you in worship." This is true. But the Lord would reply, "Then why haven't you followed my other requirements—about honesty and justice and care for the poor?" The worshipers were being terribly inconsistent, following God's worship commands, but not his living commands.

At this point, God would rather not have to put up with their hypocrisy. As Paul had told the Corinthians that their love feasts did more harm than good, so the Lord here asks them to stop the charade. The incense of their sacrifices, which once had been so pleasing (Gen. 8:21), now just stank. The word *detestable* appears about a hundred times in the Old Testament, often translated "abomination." The Lord hates it. Solomon set out to list the things that God hates. His top three: "Haughty eyes, a lying tongue, hands that shed innocent blood" (Prov. 6:17). Later he noted, "The sacrifice of the wicked is detestable" (Prov. 21:27) and, "If anyone turns a deaf ear to the law, even his prayers are detestable" (Prov. 28:9).

God indicates that the many holy days the Jews observed were weighing down on him. They were a burden. New Moon festivals may sound cultlike, but they were prescribed in God's law (Num. 28:11-15). No, there was nothing wrong with these observances in themselves. But as they droned on and on without any real meaning, God got tired of them.

"My soul hates" these wicked assemblies, God said. We don't think very much about God's "soul." Here it indicates his innermost being, that which is at the center of all he is or does. The worshipers of Judah thought they were pleasing God with all their sacrifices. But they were treating him like a machine, like some animal that you have to feed, like some dumb idol. God has a soul, which they weren't even close to. God wants a relationship with us; these worshipers apparently didn't want that. They may have thought they were touching God. But they were touching only the outside, the temple, the altar, the actions of worship. They didn't plunge any farther, to the very soul of God.

As Edward J. Young comments:

> Having abandoned a true view of the One to whom they were
> sacrificing, men placed their emphasis upon the sacrifice itself,
> and thus came to the belief that such an offering was necessary
> for God. They thus bring the offerings of their hands, but at the

116

same time withhold the integrity of their hearts. Without faith it is impossible to please God in worship or in any other aspect of life. Worship in contravention of God's commandments is no true worship, and a sacrifice offered without faith is a hollow mockery. [1]

At the peak of his reign, King Uzziah got proud. At one point, he entered the temple and approached the altar to burn incense. He was the king, but he was not a priest. And God had stipulated that only priests could serve at his altar. Eighty-one courageous priests challenged the king as he stood before the altar, and the king became angry. Suddenly, as a judgment from God, leprosy broke out on his forehead. He had to live in isolation for the rest of his life (2 Chron. 26:16-21).

In his pride, Uzziah thought he could manipulate God through ritual. It didn't work.

This story reminds us of two events in the life of another proud king, Saul. It was the custom to make sacrifices to God before going into battle. Samuel the priest had promised to come to the battle lines at Gilgal and perform the sacrifice, but he hadn't shown up yet, and Saul was getting overly anxious. The Philistines were ready for battle and Saul's men were growing impatient, so Saul did the sacrifice himself. Samuel rebuked him for disobeying the Lord's command. Saul had placed the ritual over obedience (1 Sam. 13:7-14).

Later, Saul conquered the Amalekites and was ordered to wipe them out completely. God didn't want any idol-worshipers compromising his people. Even the Amalekites' livestock was to be killed. But Saul spared the livestock "in order to sacrifice them to the LORD," as he explained to Samuel. When will this guy learn?

Samuel replied:

> Does the LORD delight in burnt offerings and sacrifices as much as in obeying the voice of the LORD? To obey is better than sacrifice, and to heed is better than the fat of rams. (1 Sam. 15:22)

That was Isaiah's message to Uzziah and to the worshipers in Judah. At about the same time, God proclaimed to Israel through Hosea: "I desire mercy, not sacrifice, and acknowledgment of God rather than burnt offerings" (Hos. 6:6). As we acknowledge that God is God, we change our ways, we follow his commands in our daily lives.

The Lord continued his admonition through Isaiah: "When you spread out your hands in prayer, I will hide my eyes from you; even if you offer many prayers, I will not listen" (Isa. 1:15). They had been treating him as a dumb idol. He would act like one.

> Your hands are full of blood; wash and make yourselves clean. Take your evil deeds out of my sight! Stop doing wrong, learn to do right! Seek justice, encourage the oppressed. Defend the cause of the fatherless, plead the case of the widow. (Isa. 1:15-17)

The blood on their hands has a double meaning. They were stained with animal blood from all their sacrifices, but they were also responsible—through neglect—for the deaths of poor people. They needed to clean up before coming to worship God. This would involve a commitment to care for the needy. But those stains would need a more powerful detergent: "'Come now, let us reason together,' says the LORD. 'Though your sins are like scarlet, they shall be as white as snow; though they are red as crimson, they shall be like wool'" (Isa. 1:18).

The cleaning comes from God himself if they will just cut through the ritual and (in Hosea's word) *acknowledge* him. They need to see him as he is. They need to deal with God's soul, not just his trappings. They need to reason together with him.

My mother has said that when we were babies, she couldn't wait for us to grow up so we could talk with her. She enjoyed each new bit of learning we received, and she "reasoned together" with us as we grew. That is a picture of God, tending these infant worshipers. At this point, all they know is that he is up there somewhere and they need to do certain things to keep him happy and get their needs met. But God longs for them to grow and see him as more than just a provider, but as a real person, with a soul. He yearns for them to reason with him.

The nineteenth-century commentator George Adam Smith put it this way:

> Although the people have silenced conscience and are steeped in a stupidity worse than ox or ass [see Isa. 1:3], God will not leave them alone. He forces himself upon them; he compels them to think. . . . God speaks to men by the reasonable words of his prophet. . . . An awakened conscience is his prophet's first

118

demand. Before religion can be prayer, or sacrifice, or any acceptable worship, it must be a reasoning together with God.[2]

God's people took the good forms of worship he had given and drained them of meaning. Even though they were bringing their grain and livestock to the altar, they were not giving God the firstfruits of their lives. There was no relation between what they did in worship and how they lived each day. The same awareness of God needs to be flowing through both activities.

The part may sanctify the whole, but it has to be a part of the whole. I may give God the first tenth of my income, but that doesn't mean I can invest the other nine-tenths in shady business deals. God sees all of my life, not just the Sunday activity. He does want me to offer part of my life and my goods to him in a special way, but that should be an indication that I recognize his claim on all my life. If I repudiate that claim Monday through Saturday, the Sunday observance becomes a lie.

This was a regular theme for many of the prophets, not just Isaiah. "Rend your heart and not your garments," Joel advised (Joel 2:13). He was referring to the ritual of repentance, tearing one's clothes. Make sure your repentance is from the heart, he said.

In Jeremiah's day, some worshipers took care to bring high-priced ingredients for the sacrifices. But God said, "What do I care about incense from Sheba or sweet calamus [an incense ingredient] from a distant land? Your burnt offerings are not acceptable; your sacrifices do not please me" (Jer. 6:20). Today he might tell the church-going property owners, "What do I care if you buy an expensive organ for the church and choir robes designed by Dior? Fix up those apartment buildings you own and stop raising the rent!"

In the next chapter, the Lord explained his discontent: "When I brought your forefathers out of Egypt . . . I did not just give them commands about burnt offerings and sacrifices, but I gave them this command: Obey me, and I will be your God and you will be my people. . . . But they did not listen or pay attention" (Jer. 7:22-24). Therefore, God didn't want their sacrificial animals. "Eat the meat yourselves," God said.

It is Amos who most closely parallels Isaiah's themes. Amos prophesied about the same time as Isaiah, but in the northern kingdom of Israel.

> I hate, I despise your religious feasts; I cannot stand your solemn assemblies. Even though you bring me burnt offerings and grain offerings, I will not accept them. Though you bring choice fellowship offerings, I will have no regard for them. Away with the noise of your songs! I will not listen to the music of your harps. But let justice roll on like a river, righteousness like a never-failing stream! (Amos 5:21-24)

Even the songs of worship rankled. They were just "noise." The Hebrew word means "commotion," "tumult," or even "multitude." The idea here is cacophony, as if everyone in your church each picked a different hymn and started singing—all at the same time. What might start out as beautiful worship becomes a mess. Just noise.

The noise God wants to hear is that of rushing waters—with the waters representing justice. The land was thirsty for justice—just as it thirsted through dry spells without rain. In those dry spells, streambeds would dry up. People would have to scramble to find water. But when the rains came, the water would flow down those mountains, filling those streambeds. Just a trickle at first; you would hear its faint gurgle. But then the current would grow. The sound would grow stronger. And soon you would have a regular river rushing by, thoroughly satisfying the needs of the parched nation. God wanted a sense of justice—of fairness and care for the needy—to sweep through the land. That was the "song of worship" he wanted to hear.

So the forms of worship really aren't important, right? It doesn't matter what we do on Sunday as long as we live well day by day, right?

Wrong.

Malachi gave quite a different picture of worship. By his time, the people weren't just going through the motions. They weren't even doing the motions very well. Malachi's rebuke indicates that it is important how we worship. The things we do in worship are expressions of where our hearts are. We need to give God good worship, not second-rate.

> "It is you, O priests, who show contempt for my name. But you ask, 'How have we shown contempt for your name?' You place defiled food on my altar. But you ask, 'How have we defiled you?' By saying that the Lord's table is contemptible. When you bring blind animals for sacrifice, is that not wrong? When you sacrifice crippled or diseased animals, is that not wrong? Try

offering them to your governor! Would he be pleased with you? Would he accept you?" says the LORD Almighty. . . . "Oh, that one of you would shut the temple doors, so that you would not light useless fires on my altar! I am not pleased with you," says the LORD Almighty, "and I will accept no offering from your hands. . . . But you profane [my name] by saying of the Lord's table, 'It is defiled,' and of its food, 'It is contemptible.' And you say, 'What a burden!' and you sniff at it contemptuously," says the LORD Almighty. . . . "Cursed is the cheat who has an acceptable male in his flock and vows to give it, but then sacrifices a blemished animal to the Lord. For I am a great king," says the LORD Almighty, "and my name is to be feared among the nations." (Mal. 1: 6-14)

Formal worship had become a "burden" to the priests of Malachi's day. The people learned to give the dregs of their produce and livestock to the Lord. It was as if the Lord didn't matter.

The Lord said, "Try that with the government!" Walter Kaiser imagines a taxpayer writing to the IRS: "Please accept this sick cow in lieu of my taxes."[3]

Of course, the priests play dumb. "What do you mean, Lord? We're observing the rituals. We're doing the sacrifices." They were pretending to be as blind as the animals they sacrificed. Apparently they thought God was blind, too.

The law was still in effect. The people knew the rules. They were supposed to give the best. But there seemed to be no one policing those rules. The laws of sacrifice became like the fifty-five-m.p.h. speed limit on most major U.S. highways. It is a nice idea, but no one really pays much attention. It was easy to slip an injured animal in the place of your prize lamb. Who would know?

God would know. And he utters a curse on the "cheat" who does this. This was much like the crime of Ananias and Sapphira in Acts 5. They pretended to give their all but gave something less. God struck them dead.

The people of Malachi's time were behaving as if God did not exist. That is the exact opposite of what worship needs to be. Worship is a celebration of God's presence. We come to him in recognition of the fact that he rules our lives. We give him our best as we commit to him our entire lives. This celebration of God's presence was sadly absent from Malachi's people.

Commentator Peter C. Craigie writes:

> Worship, properly conducted, is an expression of lives lived in the knowledge of God and in relationship with God. Worship is ordered into particular forms so that this knowledge of God may be given full and rich expression in the lives of the people. But all worship is subject to abuse from several directions. It is possible, as Amos [and Isaiah] perceived, to follow the proper forms of worship, but the worship as such be meaningless because those who worship have lost all knowledge of God. It is equally possible, as Malachi knew, for a people to be so far from God in relationship and knowledge that worship becomes virtually pointless. Nobody cared too much, for they had ceased to care about God, but they kept the old forms of worship going for the sake of tradition. They were considered unimportant, and so second-rate sacrifices were good enough to offer in worship but, when all was said and done, worship didn't matter. In both cases, problems in worship reflect deeper problems in the lives of those who worshiped. Only those who live in a continuing relationship with God can worship him in spirit and in truth.[4]

Malachi's people seem like pragmatists. What difference does it make, they ask, if the sacrificial animal is blind? The blood is shed, the ritual observed, and we get rid of a problem animal. Everybody wins. Why should I bring a tenth of my grain to the temple storerooms (see Mal. 3:10) when I could sell it, invest that money, and give some of the profits to the poor? That sounds like Judas, who suggested selling Mary's perfume-gift and giving the proceeds to the poor (John 12:5).

But God doesn't care about the bottom line. He doesn't care about the market value of the creatures brought to his altar. He cares about what's in our hearts—and the gifts we bring express what is in our hearts. In God's economic system the widow's two cents worth is of more value than the sizable donations of the wealthy (Luke 21:3). She gives her all from a heart of utter trust while the rich give what they don't need from hearts of pride.

In our modern worship, we often give God less than the best because the best costs too much. Sometimes this is for pragmatic reasons, sometimes we're just selfish.

Let us not even think about money right now but about worship. Do we invest the time to prepare for a worship service—in prayer and reading the Scripture text? Or do we come to worship exhausted from some Saturday night activity? Do we sing with all our hearts and voices? Or are we afraid what others might think? Do we volunteer to serve as ushers, Scripture readers, choir members, children's church leaders, nursery attendants? Or do we shrink from that investment of our time and energy? Do we say amen to what is said, or might that cost us our dignity? Do we invent new ways of praising God? Or might that rock the boat, offend someone?

Our "sacrifices" are different from those of Malachi's day. But the heart of worship hasn't changed. We may still be taking God for granted, showing by our actions that we don't care that much about worshiping him.

Notes

1. Edward J. Young, *The Book of Isaiah*, vol. 1 of the *New International Commentary on the Old Testament (Grand Rapids: Eerdmans, 1965), 62-3.*
2. George Adam Smith, *The Book of Isaiah*, vol. 1 (New York: A. C. Armstrong & Son, 1904), 6.
3. Walter C. Kaiser, Jr., *Malachi: God's Unchanging Love* (Grand Rapids: Baker, 1984), 40.
4. Peter C. Craigie, *Twelve Prophets*, vol. 2 of The Daily Study Bible Series (Philadelphia: Westminster Press, 1985), 233-4.

FOURTEEN
THE RIGHT WORDS
(THE PSALMS)

"I don't know how to say this, but . . ." The teenage boy's voice trails off again. His girlfriend sits patiently as the boy stammers. "I mean—I think what I'm trying to say is . . ."

Suddenly she blurts it out. "You're trying to say that you really like me and everything, but you don't want to get tied down right now, so you'd like to date other people."

He gazes in amazement. "Yeah, that's it. You know, you're amazing. You always know exactly what I'm trying to say. What would I do without you?"

She smiles coyly. "Oh, I don't know."

Knowing how to say things isn't always easy. The feelings may be there, deep within us, but how should we express them?

That is why we have greeting cards and the reason why we get things in the mail, saying, "Tell your congressman exactly what you think. Just sign this preprinted card and send it."

I sometimes write songs. More than once as I've been puzzling over the lyrics of some love ballad, I've heard on the radio some song that says everything I'm trying to say to the woman I'm crazy about. There. Why write a new one? I should just sing her that song.

Have you ever felt that way in worship? There is so much you want to say to God, but getting the right words out is a problem. You mutter the usual things: "Thank you" for this or that; "I praise you." And you

125

know God is listening—but you want to say so much more. Those phrases don't begin to vent the true feelings of your heart.

It's a mixture of feelings in there, like a rich, simmering stew. Gratitude and awe for God's greatness. A sense of inadequacy. Sorrow for sin and a desire to get things right. Anger at people who have hurt you. Maybe anger at God himself for letting some difficult things happen. Questions. An earnest desire to see God work in the lives of your loved ones. A sure faith that he can work in their lives, but also some smidgens of doubt.

The stew simmers inside you. If only you could dish up a huge bowlful of it and present it to God. But you need words to express these things. Where do you start?

Open the Psalms. Listen to David and the other sweet singers of Israel as they pour out their hearts to God. They have the words you can use.

The Psalms were the hymns of ancient Israel. Most of them were used regularly in corporate worship. That creates a certain paradox for us. The psalms obviously spring from great individual interactions with God, yet they became national treasures. They express the deep inner feeling of many of us, yet we can recite them together as a church body. As we seek to understand this paradox, we may find a needed connection between personal and corporate worship.

Singing was always a part of Israel's experience. Moses led a song by the Red Sea, Deborah sang in triumph, Hannah sang in thanksgiving for a son. Major events of national or personal life were marked by music.

But it was David who knit singing tightly into the fabric of Israel's relationship with God. He gave the nation songs to sing. He created a corps of temple singers to lead worship music. And he danced with all his might before the Lord.

The law of Moses, however, does not tell us much about singing. We are given intricate details on burnt offerings and leprosy and the dimensions of the tabernacle. But Moses doesn't say whether or when or what or how the Israelites sang in worship. We just don't know.

And the history of the Book of Psalms is uncertain. We know David wrote seventy-three of them, but others have by-lines, too, and some authors are anonymous. When were these written? We can figure that David's psalms were penned about 1000 B.C., but how soon afterward were they collected? And when were they first used in worship?

Jewish writings indicate that the Book of Psalms was used after the Babylonian Captivity, after the temple was rebuilt. Ezra may have been responsible for pulling together the final edition of the Psalter in the 400s B.C. The fact that the Psalms are divided into five "Books" indicates that these may have had separate existences in earlier periods as "hymnals" for the temple or synagogues. (Some scholars claim there were three major psalters used in Israel before Ezra collected them all. They say he made the fivefold division to mirror the five books of Moses.)

All of that scholarly guesswork may not matter to us much now—except for one key question: What is the nature of these psalms? Are they written as private soul-stirrings or public anthems? Are they more like diary entries or Top Forty hits?

Looking at the psalms themselves, we find inklings of both. We can almost feel the pastureland beneath us as we read Psalm 23. It doesn't take too much to imagine the shepherd-boy David composing these lines as he reclined by the "still waters," watching his sheep drink. Yet many of the psalms are set in a context of public worship. The antiphonal form of some psalms suggests congregational responses. In fact the general parallelism of nearly every psalm would fit very nicely into a statement-response format in a public assembly. This all makes me think that David and the other psalmists were intentionally writing for public worship—even while they distilled their very personal thoughts and feelings.

I have led my church in prayer on occasion. It is an interesting experience. It turns out to be a personal, heartfelt prayer—but it's quite different from the prayers I pray when I'm alone with God. I am praying not only from myself but on behalf of the entire church. Naturally, I leave out the specifically personal things I might pray about. I don't say, "Lord, I'm really sorry about that fight with Jack—and I confess I looked lustfully at Janet this morning." Instead, I pray, "Lord, we are sorry for the sins we have committed against you." I assume each person will fill in his or her own fights and lustful glances. I don't pray, "Lord, help me to finish my article for *Christian History Magazine.*" I pray, "Lord, we come with various needs that we know you can fill. Help us all to serve you in the work we do."

The Psalms are like that, too. As personal as they are, they don't name names. They don't overflow with specific situations from the psalmist's life. The Psalms use various metaphors to express situations that many people can relate to: "My enemies are tormenting me," or "You have really helped me this time, Lord," or "I'm depressed."

This indicates that they were written not only from personal experience but with the intention of sharing that experience with a whole congregation. David and the other psalmists wrote lyrics that people could sing with them. The psalmists' struggles match our struggles. We easily fit our own needs and fears into David's prayers. And often, very often, he finds the words we cannot find to express our souls to God.

Let me suggest three major things we can learn about worship from the Psalms. These are certainly not the only things to learn. The Book of Psalms is rich with praises, and the true student of worship should immerse himself in this deep pool. But here are some ideas you may not have thought of, some things that need saying.

1. *The range of emotions and attitudes in the Psalms suggests that we should come more honestly to the Lord in worship.* The psalmists ran the gamut, from elation to despair. Many of the things the psalmists say would be judged inappropriate in our churches. We have mastered the religion of "niceness." When David crumbles in despair or calls for the destruction of his enemies or wonders why God has forsaken him, we would shush him. "Don't say that, David. That's not nice."

And yet there it is, in the Bible. The psalmists do not say that this is a good way to feel or think or talk—but they do feel that way. And where better to express those feelings but before the Lord?

David was once described as "a man after God's own heart" (1 Sam. 13:14). Of course, this means that he shared the Lord's feelings and passions, but I've always liked that word *after*. I picture David chasing after God's heart, longing to feel as God feels. His psalms, then, give us the chase scene. "Here's how I feel, Lord. How should I feel?" "How about now, Lord? Am I getting any closer?"

As the deer pants for streams of water, so my soul pants for you, O God. My soul thirsts for God, for the living God. When can I go and meet with God? My tears have been my food day and night, while men say to me all day long, "Where is your God?" These things I remember as I pour out my soul: how I used to go with the multitude, leading the procession to the house of God, with shouts of joy and thanksgiving among the festive throng. Why are you downcast, O my soul? Why so disturbed within me? Put your hope in God, for I will yet praise him, my Savior and my God. (Ps. 42:1-5)

Here, as in a number of his psalms, David seemed to change the subject halfway through. "Things are lousy . . ." and he recited them, one after another—and suddenly, "Put your hope in the Lord! He is great!" It is not schizophrenia; it is a change of perspective. If you were filming a chase scene, you would show the lead car, then the chasing car, then you would cut to the lead car again. This is David's "cut" to a picture of God. "I'm still chasing after your heart, Lord, but I know you're there. Thanks."

David knew that you can't learn if you try to hide your needs from the teacher. How many of us have tried that in school—pretending to know something that we really haven't the foggiest notion of? We just wanted to get a good grade, to impress the teacher, when we should have admitted our ignorance and learned. One wise teacher of mine once said, "There's no such thing as a dumb question. If you have a question about something I'm teaching, ask it. The dumbest thing is not to ask."

And so David presented his needs openly and honestly before the Lord. He was not arrogant. He knew he needed help. And by launching these sentiments to the Lord, he was taking the right first step.

Praise the LORD, O my soul; all my inmost being, praise his holy name. Praise the LORD, O my soul, and forget not all his benefits. He forgives all your sins and heals all your diseases. (Ps. 103:1-3)

We love this. When we say, "The Psalms teach us how to worship," this is what we have in mind. We have this image of worship as being a close, warm feeling of fellowship with God. As it often is.

But, as we have been studying Scripture, we have been learning that worship is much broader than that. We might define it as "meeting with God." The Lord often fills us with warm feelings of being loved, but sometimes there are problems. Sometimes there is sin in our lives. Sometimes we are unconsciously putting up walls. Sometimes, as with Job, we just don't know why, but God seems far away—maybe he is testing our faith. The worst thing we can do is to pretend that everything is all right with God when it isn't. Most of us try to do this. We try to manufacture a "worship experience," when God just wants us to meet with him as we are.

> You have put me in the lowest pit, in the darkest depths. Your wrath lies heavily upon me; you have overwhelmed me with all your waves. You have taken from me my closest friends and have made me repulsive to them. I am confined and cannot escape; my eyes are dim with grief. . . . Why, O LORD, do you reject me and hide your face from me? (Ps. 88:6-9, 14)

In a strange way, this is worship, too. No warm fuzzies, just an honest heart-to-heart with God. Only by admitting that we feel like this can we ever rely fully on the Lord to lift us up. And he will.

When we allow ourselves to sing Psalm 88 one week, we may be singing Psalm 40 the next Sunday:

> I waited patiently for the LORD; he turned to me and heard my cry. He lifted me out of the slimy pit, out of the mud and mire; he set my feet on a rock and gave me a firm place to stand. He put a new song in my mouth, a hymn of praise to our God. Many will see and fear and put their trust in the LORD. (Ps. 40:1-3)

2. *The range of situations in the Psalms gives us a wide range of reasons to praise the Lord.* When it comes right down to it, we usually only praise part of God. When we pick and choose the psalms that form our worship, we needlessly limit our understanding of the God we're praising.

Our God is Creator, Provider, Deliverer, Strength, and Shield. He is our Mighty Fortress, our Help in Ages Past, our Shepherd. That is what we like to praise God for. But God is also a Vengeful Warrior, a Just Judge, the Awesome One Who Hides Himself, the One Who Tries People's Souls, the Sufferer. Because God is all this and more, we can worship him in any situation. If we fail to recognize this, we run the risk of worshiping a God made in our image.

Walter Brueggemann has suggested a simple but comprehensive scheme for understanding the varied situations of the Psalms. The Psalms, he says, can be divided into "poems of orientation, poems of disorientation, and poems of new orientation."[1] Brueggemann explained, "The flow of human life characteristically is located either in the actual experience of one of these settings, or is in movement from one to another."

Psalms of orientation reflect times of well-being. These songs "articulate the joy, delight, goodness, coherence, and reliability of God, God's creation, God's governing law," Brueggemann said.

> Great is the LORD and most worthy of praise; his greatness no one can fathom. One generation will commend your works to another; they will tell of your mighty acts. They will speak of the glorious splendor of your majesty, and I will meditate on your wonderful works. They will tell of the power of your awesome works, and I will proclaim your great deeds. They will celebrate your abundant goodness and joyfully sing of your righteousness. (Ps. 145:3-7)

This psalm speaks of God's mighty acts and the community that praises him for these acts. There is a tight relationship here between God and his people. Everything is in order. (The order is even indicated by the alphabetical structure of the psalm: the first verse starts with the Hebrew *A*, the second with the Hebrew *B*, and so on.) All is well with the world. (*All* is a key word in the psalm, used over a dozen times.)

Psalm 33 expresses more of this good feeling: "The LORD loves righteousness and justice; the earth is full of his unfailing love" (v. 5). God has showered his blessings upon his creation and deserves our worship. "It is fitting for the upright to praise him" (v. 1). It just makes sense. When we praise, we are just doing what is appropriate, what we are meant to do.

Psalms 8, 104, and others further celebrate God's creation. We find our orientation as created beings, blessed by God and returning praises. Psalms 1, 5, 24, and 119 honor God as the giver of the law. We find our orientation as recipients of that law, students of his Word. Things go well when we obey what he says. Other psalms speak of God's wisdom (14, 37) or justice (112) or loving sovereignty (131, 133)—principles by which the world works. We may find orientation as we act wisely, rely on his justice, or love others.

Psalms of disorientation spring from times of hurt, alienation, suffering, and death. These evoke rage, resentment, self-pity, and hatred. These are the tough psalms, the despairing psalms, the nasty psalms.

They generally begin with a plea for deliverance from a bad situation. God is addressed rather personally, the situation is described and God is begged to act.

> How long, O LORD? Will you forget me forever? How long will you hide your face from me? How long must I wrestle with my thoughts and every day have sorrow in my heart? How long will my enemy triumph over me? Look on me and answer, O LORD my God. (Ps. 13:1-3)

> Hear, O LORD, and answer me, for I am poor and needy. Guard my life, for I am devoted to you. You are my God; save your servant who trusts in you. (Ps. 86:1-2)

Sometimes the psalmist tries to talk God into rescuing him—by repenting, by declaring his innocence, by promising to praise him, by telling him how bad it is for his (God's) reputation to allow this suffering, by reminding God of previous times of rescue.

> Give light to my eyes, or I will sleep in death; my enemy will say, "I have overcome him," and my foes will rejoice when I fall. (Ps. 13:3-4)

> Give ear to my prayer—it does not rise from deceitful lips. . . . Though you test me, you will find nothing; I have resolved that my mouth will not sin. (Ps. 17:1, 3)

> I confess my iniquity; I am troubled by my sin. . . . Come quickly to help me, O LORD my Savior. (Ps. 38:18, 22)

> How long will the enemy mock you, O God? Will the foe revile your name forever? . . . But you, O God, are my king from of old; you bring salvation upon the earth. It was you who split open the sea by your power. (Ps. 74:10, 12)

Sometimes the plea even includes a hateful prayer for retribution against the psalmist's enemies.

> Arise, O LORD! Deliver me, O my God! Strike all my enemies on the jaw; break the teeth of the wicked. (Ps 3:7)

> May all who gloat over my distress be put to shame and confusion; may all who exalt themselves over me be clothed with shame and disgrace. (Ps. 35:26)

But almost always the plea turns a corner and becomes praise.

> But I trust in your unfailing love; my heart rejoices in your salvation. I will sing to the LORD, for he has been good to me. (Ps. 13:5-6)

> You are forgiving and good, O LORD, abounding in love to all who call to you. (Ps. 86:5)

Some of the Psalms (74, 79, 137) are communal laments, following similar patterns.

"Why have you rejected us forever, O God? Why does your anger smolder against the sheep of your pasture?" Note that the psalmist sometimes blamed himself for his troubles: he has sinned, but he was repenting and begging God for mercy. Sometimes he blamed his enemies: he himself was an innocent victim, and he begged God to stand on the side of righteousness. Sometimes he blamed God: for some mysterious reason, God has rejected him, and he begged God to accept him again.

Through it all, God is seen as worthy of praise. He is praised for his mercy in receiving a repentant sinner. He is praised for his justice and power, seen in both the vengeance he wreaks on unrighteous foes and the rescue of his faithful ones. He is praised for his mysterious "aboveness." The psalmist may not have understood what God was doing to him, but he still trusted that God was worthy of praise. In this he was like Job, who said: "The LORD gave and the LORD has taken away; may the name of the LORD be praised" (Job 1:21).

Psalms of new orientation come from those times. Brueggemann wrote, "When we are overwhelmed with the new gifts of God, then joy breaks through the despair. Where there has been darkness, there is light."

> I will exalt you, O LORD, for you lifted me out of the depths and did not let my enemies gloat over me. O LORD my God, I called to you for help and you healed me. O LORD, you brought me up from the grave; you spared me from going down into the pit.

Sing to the LORD, you saints of his; praise his holy name. For his anger lasts only a moment, but his favor lasts a lifetime; weeping may remain for a night, but rejoicing comes in the morning. . . . You turned my wailing into dancing; you removed my sackcloth and clothed me with joy, that my heart may sing to you and not be silent. O LORD my God, I will give you thanks forever. (Ps. 30:1-5, 11-12)

Notice the sense of past, present, and future. The Lord saved me in the past. I begged him to help, and he helped me. Therefore I am singing now, and encouraging others to sing. This will be the constant pattern of my life forever—to praise and thank the Lord.

This is the calm after the battle, the postgame interview. You can almost hear the psalmist sighing—the hard times are over. But it is also an inauguration address. There is a sense of newness. Things will be different around here. New life is just beginning, and it will be a life of praise. (The psalm was used as a dedication for the temple, according to its subtitle. This new temple was certainly a "new orientation" for Israel's worship.)

Psalm 99 speaks of God as a triumphant king. He will reign with justice. It speaks of Moses, Aaron and Samuel calling on the Lord to help Israel in times of need.

O LORD our God, you answered them; you were to Israel a forgiving God, though you punished their misdeeds. Exalt the LORD our God and worship at his holy mountain, for the LORD our God is holy. (Ps. 99:8-9)

Forgiveness has been extended. Now, back in fellowship with God, we can exalt him in holiness.

These three categories of the Psalms give us three major aspects of God to worship. In the first, he is Creator, Lawgiver, Just Judge. In the second, he is both the angry God who demands holiness and the Suffering Servant who makes us holy. In the third, he is the Redeemer of our lives and the world's conquering King.

Our worship can reflect this progression. Too often we have stayed with the initial orientation, afraid to admit any spiritual disarray, and thus have deprived ourselves of the full joy of redemption. When we sing only the "happy songs," we neglect not only the laments but also the rugged songs of triumph.

134

Brueggemann commented, "It is a curious fact that the church has, by and large, continued to sing songs of orientation in a world increasingly experienced as disoriented." He allows that this may reflect a defiant faith but guesses that it is more likely "a frightened, numb denial and deception that does not want to acknowledge or experience the disorientation of life." He attributes it less to our faith and more to the "wishful optimism of our culture." It is clear, he says, that "a church that goes on singing 'happy songs' in the face of raw reality is doing something very different from what the Bible itself does." The "psalms of darkness," as he calls them, do not demonstrate failure or lack of faith but a bold, transformed faith—one that recognizes the disarray of our lives and trusts God to fix it.[2] Can we show this in our worship services? Our call to worship and initial hymns of praise might reflect our delight (and orientation) in God's created order, in his Word, and in God himself. But then we can grasp our disorientation by confessing our sins, decrying the injustice in our society, and praying for the healing of hurting individuals and broken situations. We can then find new orientation as we thank God for past victories and trust him for future ones, committing ourselves to live according to his new regime. The Psalms can instruct our worship at each stage (as can the rest of Scripture: the sermon could fit in at any stage of this worship scheme).

3. *The corporate aspect of the Psalms suggests that we can be more open with each other, supporting each other through difficult and happy times.* As we have said, the Psalmist was not just speaking for his own benefit. The Psalms have rich application to the communal life—and worship—of God's people.

Note the experience of the psalmist Asaph:

> This is what the wicked are like—always carefree, they increase in wealth. Surely in vain have I kept my heart pure; in vain have I washed my hands in innocence. All day long I have been plagued; I have been punished every morning. If I had said, "I will speak thus," I would have betrayed your children. When I tried to understand all this, it was oppressive to me till I entered the sanctuary of God; then I understood their final destiny. Surely you place them on slippery ground; you cast them down to ruin. (Ps. 73:12-18)

Asaph doubted that righteousness was worth the trouble. This is the kind of talk we don't like to hear in church. We don't want doubts expressed; church is a place for faith. If we had our way, Asaph would never show up in the sanctuary. Or, if he did, he'd keep quiet about his spiritual struggle.

Asaph recognized his responsibility not to proclaim his doubts as gospel truth ("I will speak thus"). That might lead others astray. This is what we, too, are afraid of in our churches. But Asaph did express his doubt *as doubt* here in this Psalm.

When he entered the sanctuary, then he understood. He gained God's perspective. Presumably there were others worshiping in the sanctuary, too. It was not just his presence before God that opened his eyes but his participation with other worshipers. In the words and deeds of worship, the truth becomes clear. Righteousness is worth it, in the long run.

So the community can lead one through a struggle; it can also be the recipient of the good news of a struggle that has been won. The first twenty-one verses of Psalm 22 present an agonizing struggle. The Gospel writers applied some of these verses to Jesus' ordeal on the cross. But in verse 22 it turns the corner into praise and includes the entire congregation:

> I will declare your name to my brothers; in the congregation I will praise you. . . . From you comes the theme of my praise in the great assembly; before those who fear you will I fulfill my vows. (Ps. 22:22, 25)

That last phrase captures another aspect of the community's involvement in personal struggles. The group witnesses one's "vows"— that is, one's commitment to honor God in the future. We hold each other accountable to keep the promises we make to God as we worship.

As mentioned earlier, the Psalms also include community struggles of faith. "By the rivers of Babylon we sat and wept"—so begins Psalm 137. It's an expression of the national sorrow of Jews in captivity. Our churches might experience similar struggles—a near church split, perhaps; a scandal of some kind; a financial crisis; the loss of someone very dear to the whole congregation. The Psalms enable us not only to support each other in personal crises but also to give expressions to the feelings in our hearts during group crises such as these.

We do pretty well with group expressions of praise. But the Psalms show us a wide range of situations and emotions. We should not lock these out of the worship service. We should embrace them, work through them with the psalmists, and emerge proclaiming the mighty victories of God.

Notes

1. Walter Brueggemann, *The Message of the Psalms* (Minneapolis: Augsburg, 1984), 19ff.
2. ———, 51-52.

FIFTEEN

WORSHIP IS FOR GOD

We must radically redirect our thinking about worship.

Up to this point, we have been searching through Scripture, trying to get a feel for biblical worship. We have drawn numerous lessons along the way. We have gathered clues and nuances about this crucial concept. From these Scriptures, seven principles can be distilled.

The first of these principles is very basic, but essential: *Worship is for God.* Too often, people come to a worship service hoping to "get something out of it." One of the highest compliments we can pay a worship service, it seems, is: "I was blessed."

What is wrong with that? Shouldn't we expect to get something out of a service? Is it wrong to feel "blessed"?

Expectations are fine; and God does bless us richly when we commune with him. The problem has to do with our goals. What are we really trying to do when we worship? If our main aim is to "get something out of it," we are missing the point. We can manufacture all sorts of experiences to inspire our own hearts. Some worship planners and worship leaders are experts at massaging the emotions of their parishioners. A majestic anthem, a dramatic reading, a contemplative song sung a capella—and suddenly the congregation is riding an emotional high. But is God being worshiped? The whole event can easily become an expression of a certain spiritual hedonism. We seek our own religious pleasure.

The lines of distinction are delicate here. How can you tell a hedonistic service from a truly worshipful one? You may not be able to see any difference. The difference is in the hearts of the worshipers, in their motivations. The difference is a matter of direction.

The true worshiper aims his or her worship toward God. The act of worship is completed when God receives the worship. As a result of this worship, the worshiper receives blessings. That is just the way God is. He gives and gives, and any personal interaction with him yields benefits.

The selfish worshiper, however, counts on those "return" blessings. He or she also aims worship toward God, but the act is not really completed until the return blessings are received. This worshiper judges the success of the worship on the basis of those return blessings. So if he feels very blessed, it must have been very good worship. If she does not get anything out of it, it must not have been good worship.

You can go crazy trying to slice your motivations just right. There is an element of self-interest in most everything we do. A young man may tell his beloved, "I love you because you make me feel so good." And that may be enough, for a while. But in any relationship the times come when she doesn't make him feel good, when it is downright painful, or at least inconvenient, to do loving things. True love proves itself when the crunch comes.

True worship may be like that, too. For a while it may be fine to exult in the blessings we receive from blessing God. As we have already indicated, there is nothing wrong with enjoying the gifts God returns to us. But a selfish attitude toward worship can betray itself in several ways.

1. *Leaders as performers.* We live in an entertainment society. It is natural for us to fit worship into that mold. Thus our worship leaders—the pastor, song leader, choir, other musicians—are seen as entertainers. Their job, according to this false view of worship, is to please the congregation—or at least to make them feel "worshipful." The congregation is an audience, passive, receptive.

But Scripture depicts God as the audience. The worshipers are the "entertainers," if you will, called to do a command performance for the King of kings. The worship leaders are just that, leading the worship that is offered by the congregation.

2. *The tyranny of personal taste.* The performance view of worship leads to other problems. Worship becomes very individualistic. I begin

to judge the worship on the basis of what I like. I fail to see myself as part of the body of Christ, the worshiping congregation. If a soloist sings something I don't like, I am not entertained, therefore I do not worship. In fact, I may be a bit angry with the soloist or the music planner for interfering with my worship experience.

But if I see worship as a giving of gifts to the Lord, I can affirm the gift of that soloist. Whether or not it is "my kind of music," I can appreciate the diversity of the church body, and say amen to the soloist's act of worship.

3. *Limitations in planning.* Because of this tyranny of personal taste, leaders learn not to plan activities or music that the majority of people won't like. A certain song may beautifully embody the message of the day's text, but if it has too much of a rock beat, forget it. The day's Scripture passage may just cry out for a dramatic reading, but are the people "ready" for that? If the major question asked by worship planners is, "Will the people like this?" the direction of that church's worship is all wrong.

The central question should be, What does God like? That is not always an easy question to answer, but that must be where the worship planning starts.

4. *Manipulation.* Not only do leaders learn what they can't get away with in a worship service, they also learn what people like. They learn how to get the congregation "in the mood." Some leaders meticulously craft a worship service to push all the right emotional buttons. Churches are often very enthusiastic about such services. The people feel great.

The problem with this approach is that it treats worship as merely an emotion. Worship is an action. We must hurry to add that the action of worship is properly motivated by an attitude of worship, and this attitude should have some emotional components. Our awareness of God's greatness may fill us with joy or awe or remorse. But these emotions are not the finish line. They must propel us into actions of celebration and commitment. Actions alone, unpropelled by an attitude of worship, also fall short of God's desires—the prophets rebuked the Israelites for sacrificing with hard hearts. But the emotions alone are also inadequate. It is not enough to feel; we must express.

An acting student was working on a scene from *Hamlet.* He was working hard at "getting into character." He studied the script, he explored the background of the prince of Denmark, he did improvisations with the other actors, he thought a lot about what Hamlet must have been feeling and thinking when he uttered his famous "To be or not to be." And then he performed the scene—very badly. After the instructor gently but soundly criticized the performance, the student spoke up. "I don't understand," he said. "I just don't see how it could have been so bad. You see, I really felt like Hamlet on that stage. I felt his feelings, I thought his thoughts. I was Hamlet. Isn't that enough?"

The professor thought a moment and replied, "If you were the only person in the room, that might be enough. But you have an audience. If actors acted only for their own benefit, that might be enough. Acting might be a very therapeutic self-help method. But we act for an audience. Everything we have, we must give to them. They must see what we feel.

"It is good to feel the character's feelings. You have done your homework well. But you must learn to express those feelings in honest ways, so the audience can share in them. As I watched you, I could tell that you were being very emotional. But you were concentrating so much on your own emotions that you never gave anything to the audience. The only emotion we felt was envy because there seemed to be something important going on inside of you, but we had no idea what it was."

Many worshipers are like that actor, focusing on their own emotional experience. God is the audience. We must give to him. It is great to feel those emotions in worship, but we must learn to express them to God.

5. *Cheap substitutes.* When emotions of worship are our final goal, we can easily settle for cheap substitutes. Many of the emotions aroused in our worship services are not responses to God at all but are aesthetic responses to the beauty of our own worship. We can close our eyes and sway to an a capella "Alleluia" and attain a great high without focusing on the Lord at all.

The answer is not to discourage emotion, but to follow through on it. Express those emotions in actions of worship and keep sending the worship toward God.

6. *Limitation of response to God.* Worship shouldn't always make us feel good. Sometimes our encounter with God should shake us by the shoulders and say, "Shape up!" Sometimes worship should involve times of sober commitment, sometimes sorrow for our sin.

When we tailor our worship experiences to meet our own needs, we can easily favor the positive emotions and ignore the more difficult responses to God. When we aim to "get a blessing" from a worship service, we will be less apt to examine our own lives critically and make hard choices.

7. *"Resultiness."* One final drawback of selfish worship requires some explanation—and another acting analogy. My college theater professor would sometimes criticize actors for being "resulty." This meant that they were playing for effect. They were trying to get a laugh from the audience rather than being true to the character. The professor acknowledged that you could get more laughs (or sobs) by "mugging" here and there, but you would lose so much more in the process. You would sabotage the truth of the character. The character would be less human, more of a caricature, someone the audience could laugh at but not identify with. To treat a play with integrity, the professor insisted, you had to concentrate on presenting the character as truthfully as possible and not worry about results. We would just have to trust that the fuller depiction of the character would have a deeper and more valuable (though perhaps less vocal) effect on the audience.

In a way, this is the opposite problem from that of the acting student who did Hamlet. The student didn't express; the "resulty" actor expresses too much.

Is it wrong to want the audience to enjoy the show? And, drawing the analogy, if God is our audience, is it wrong to want him to enjoy our worship? Certainly not. But what is the "resulty" actor really doing? The "resulty" actor feeds on feedback from the audience—he wants the big laugh. Never mind the fact that he may ruin a bigger laugh later, he still mugs for the laugh now. Never mind the fact that he may detract from the audience's overall enjoyment (and perhaps their deep-felt appreciation and involvement), he has to hear that applause now in order to feel that he is doing OK. So the "resulty" actor is not really giving to the audience, but using them as a mirror. He bounces his jokes off them; they laugh; he gets his strokes.

I don't want to be too hard on "resulty" actors. I've known plenty. They are not totally self-serving. A part of them really desires to please the audience. But they don't trust in the process; they don't rely on the truth of the play to move an audience in deep (and maybe quiet) ways.

In the same way, we can be "resulty" in worship. We may think we are trying to please God, but we don't trust the process. We subtly change what we do in order to get the vibes back from God. We begin "mugging" for ourselves, doing what pleases us, rather than truly worshiping God.

We may believe that worship should express the gifts of the body of Christ, but we would much rather import a skilled soloist than listen to a church member who is not quite so gifted. Yes, there are other issues involved there—"quality" in worship, for instance—but how much of our preference is based on our desire to craft the best "worship experience" for our own enjoyment?

We read that we should "sing a new song to the Lord," but we keep choosing the old favorites. Why? Because it is so hard to "worship" with the new unfamiliar tunes. And some of them don't fit our favorite styles. What we mean is that it is hard for us to "feel worshipful" with new songs. So, rather than trusting the process of worship and obeying Scripture, we stick with songs that make us feel good.

Time for a disclaimer. I believe that most believers worship with mixed motives. It is only natural. And it may not be entirely bad. We give and God gives back, and we shouldn't try to dissect the whole thing beyond recognition. It is possible to be so self-conscious about one's motives in worship that worship never takes place. Don't let that happen.

Trying to worship is like watching the needle on a car's fuel gauge. It points toward full and, as I drive, it slowly inches toward empty. I need to see when it is pointing the wrong way and then pull into the gas station and change its direction. So with worship, we may start out directing our worship toward God. But the natural tendency is to begin focusing more and more on ourselves, on our experience of worship. The arrow gravitates away from God and toward ourselves. We need to see when that is happening, and how bad it is, and then redirect the arrow by refocusing on God.

144

SIXTEEN
WORSHIP IS A GIVING OF OUR FIRSTFRUITS

"I don't need to go to church to worship. I can worship God anywhere—on a beach, in a park, in my room."

Chances are you have heard that or something like it. And it is true. God's presence is not confined to our buildings. This was part of what Jesus was saying to the Samaritan woman (John 4) and what Paul told the Athenian philosophers (Acts 17).

"I believe your whole life should be worship. I worship God as much on a day-to-day basis as I do on Sunday. So I don't really need to go to church, do I?"

Well . . . This is sort of true, too. In some sense, our whole lives should be lived with a sense of God's presence and of our commitment to him. We should praise and thank him regularly, continually.

Does that mean it is not important to go to church?

No, we usually reply, we still need to meet together with other believers—for fellowship, if for nothing else. And the church service can help us worship God. The songs inspire us and the sermon teaches us how to live day by day.

This is true, too, but I don't think it is the best answer. I think we need to make two distinctions. First, there is a difference between one's *individual* worship and the church's *corporate* worship. We will talk about that in the next chapter.

In this chapter, let us consider the difference between *general* worship and *special* worship. General worship is the day-to-day life

145

that pleases God. Special worship consists of those times that we set aside in a special way to worship God.

Our special worship times are the "firstfruits" of our lives of general worship. Remember that the Israelites brought the first portion of their crops and livestock to the altar to present to God in a special way. By doing this, they indicated that they knew God owned all of their crops and herds. The special offering dedicated the entire (general) amount. By giving the small part in a special way, they showed their desire to give God the whole thing in a general way—to enjoy their wealth in ways that would honor and please God. But it didn't always work that way, leading us to our first major requirement of special worship.

Special worship must grow out of a life of general worship. The prophets inform us that the people drove a wedge between special worship and general worship. They continued to perform the sacrifices while flagrantly violating God's laws. Thus their sacrifices were lies. In the act of bringing their best livestock for sacrifice, they were saying, "Here's the best part, Lord, as a representative of my entire estate. Take this as a token of my desire to use all my goods for your glory." And then they used the rest of their wealth to exploit the poor; they abused God's laws about land and employment in order to amass greater fortunes. The very crops they presented were probably grown on land they had stolen from widows.

They were breaking that necessary connection between special worship and general life-worship.

Paul later affirmed this connection by begging the Romans to present their bodies as "living sacrifices." Their daily lives needed to be "holy, acceptable to God" (Rom. 12:1). Yet the early church was not forsaking special worship. They continued to meet together to honor the Lord. In fact, since Romans 12:1 is followed by instructions about the church body, it might be argued that Paul intended the very presentation of those "living sacrifices" to take place in a church service. That is, as part of the church's worship, people would commit themselves fully to God, promising to live holy lives. That special-worship promise would be fulfilled by a general-worship life-style.

Special worship celebrates the special presence of Christ. Consider the question: Where is Jesus? There are at least five right answers.

Ask a five-year-old in Sunday school, and he will point up. Jesus is in heaven. Biblical theology confirms this: he is at the right hand of God, poised to return to earth, gather his people, and establish his kingdom.

Ask a nine-year-old, and she might point to herself. Jesus is in her heart. Yes, through his Spirit, he lives inside us. Our bodies are temples of that Spirit. He guides our actions, whispering directions as we walk through life.

Ask a college student who is on a social consciousness kick, and he will spread his arms and say Jesus is in the lives of the poor and dispossessed. This, too, has merit. Jesus said, "Whatever you did for one of the least of these brothers of mine, you did for me" (Matt. 25:40).

Now we get into the areas that relate to special worship.

Ask a Baptist pastor, and he will spread his arms to the congregation. Jesus is here when we meet together. He promised, "Where two or three come together in my name, there am I with them" (Matt. 18:20). Paul carried the idea farther, calling the church the body of Christ.

Ask an Anglican priest, and he will spread his arms to the Lord's Table. Jesus is here in the Eucharist. Being Anglican, he is not anxious to define just *how* Christ is present, but Jesus had said, "This is my body." Various Christian traditions take that various ways. Catholics say a physical transformation takes place; Anglicans say it is a mystery, but Christ is "really" present; Baptists tend to say Christ makes his presence felt in our hearts as we commemorate his death for us. It can all get confusing, but we would all agree in the most general terms: Christ is present with us in some way as we partake of the Lord's Supper.

So we have at least five "presences" of Christ. Is he any more present with two or three than with just me? Well, no. But he is present in a different way, a special way.

What we are calling "general worship" is the Christian's daily celebration of Christ's presence in his or her life. Because Christ is in our hearts, guiding our lives by his Spirit, we honor him with holy, worshipful lives.

But this "special worship" on Sunday celebrates Christ's special "two or three" presence. When we meet together in his name, we form his body. It is not just the collection of his "presences" in each individual. He is there with us in a special way, in our interaction with each other. That is what we celebrate.

And that gives us the guiding question for our worship services. We have an "audience" with Christ the King, our beloved Savior. What should we do? We will talk more about the answers to this question in

147

the following chapters, but we need to begin thinking about worship in this way.

Yes, Christ is present in each one of us. We certainly need to be considering what he thinks of how we live each day. But, in this special way, he is going to be in your church on Sunday. This Sunday. Your church. How does that make you feel?

If the rock group Bon Jovi were appearing at the Deptford Mall on Sunday, teenage girls for miles around would be eagerly awaiting. They would be buying new clothes and teasing their hair and making little cards and gifts to give their idols.

Should we do less for Jesus?

OK, maybe we don't need to tease our hair quite as much, but that is what "special worship" is all about—the special celebration of Christ's special presence with us. The magi learned that the King of the Jews would be appearing in a Bethlehem stall. They traveled miles, bearing expensive gifts. Giving up whatever decorum they may have had, they knelt before a little baby. That was special worship.

Special worship must be special. This is what Malachi wrote about. People were "sacrificing" crippled animals, rotting grain. They were neglecting both special worship and general obedience. The law had stipulated that God be given the best, the first. They were presenting leftovers.

It's not a matter of buying God's favor. It is an expression of what is in our hearts. If we give him shoddy stuff, it shows we don't "care enough to give the very best."

Our very forms of worship can be seen as offerings of "firstfruits." We meet on Sunday, the first day of the week. This commemorates the resurrection of Jesus, who was the "firstfruits" of those who had died (1 Cor. 15:20). That is, God will raise all believers, but he raised Christ first, as his special promise that the ultimate redemption of the dead will eventually follow.

For many of us, Sunday can also be seen as the "best" day of the week. Those with Monday-to-Friday jobs often do errands on Saturday and relax on Sunday. I was just talking with people at one church about beginning a Saturday night service. It was mentioned that some might appreciate the opportunity to attend on Saturday so they wouldn't have to "mess up" their Sunday. That is exactly the wrong attitude. If Sunday is the best day of the week, that is what we should give God for our special worship.

148

We generally wear our best clothes to the worship service. There is no Scripture commanding this, but it is appropriate. Certainly we can be just as worshipful in jeans, but we want to give God the firstfruits of our wardrobe.

We give God the best sounds we can make. (This may get kind of artsy, but stay with it.) We make lots of sounds during the week: words and yells and hems and haws. But on Sunday we sing. Singing is good sound; sustained, ordered sound from the same voices that hem and haw. We give God those good sounds in worship, even as we commit ourselves to honor God with our weekday words.

Then, in most churches, the choir is the firstfruits of the congregation. These are the best singers, selected to make exceptionally good sounds, special sounds, for God's glory. The song they sing is a gift from the entire congregation, since they are the "first portion" (musically) of the entire church.

If churches have processions or sacred dance, these can be seen as firstfruits of the movements we make during the week.

And, of course, in the offering we give the firstfruits of our income.

Since worship is our giving of firstfruits, we must make sure that we are giving God our best. *Our* best. You do not need to sing like Pavarotti, but you do need to practice. We all need to prepare our hearts and our gifts so that we truly honor God in our special worship.

SEVENTEEN
CHURCH WORSHIP
IS CORPORATE

There is such a thing as personal worship. Moments of meditation and prayer bring many Christians before God on a daily basis. He is present with them in a special way through his Spirit. He draws near to them as they draw near to him.

And the Bible teems with stories of such individual worship: Moses in Midian, Elijah by the brook, the child Samuel saying, "Speak, Lord," Isaiah with the cherubim, Jesus in the Garden, Peter on the rooftop, Paul caught up to the "third heaven."

Throughout history, God has dealt with individuals. But he has also dealt with groups—the nation of Israel, the church. The Israelites continually met with God in times of special worship to renew their covenant with him. "We are your people. You are our God." As we have seen, the early church met together to do much the same thing.

Individual Israelites could meditate on God's goodness and feel close to him, but their relationship with God sprang from the fact that they were Israelites. The corporate relationship led to their personal relationships with God.

The New Testament emphasizes the individual more. The tongues of fire at Pentecost separated and hovered over each of the individual believers there. God's Spirit dwells in the hearts of individual Christians. But the Bible never loses sight of the importance of the group. The church is called the "Israel of God" (Gal. 6:16). The church is

Christ's body. The church is the "temple of the Holy Spirit" (1 Cor. 3:16).

You may not know that verse. Yet you probably do know the verse a few chapters later where Paul said to individual Christians, "Do you not know that your body is a temple of the Holy Spirit?" (1 Cor. 6:19). Paul was warning against sexual immorality. In modern times, evangelicals have used this verse to condemn drinking, smoking, and other vices. We are well aware of our personal responsibilities as Christians. We know God lives in our individual bodies.

But in 1 Corinthians 3, Paul used much the same language to guard against divisions in the church: "Don't you know that you yourselves are God's temple and that God's Spirit lives in you [plural]? . . . God's temple is sacred, and you [plural] are that temple" (1 Cor. 3:16-17).

Part of what it means to be a Christian is to be "one of the Christians." Suddenly I am an arm or an eye in a larger body. I can relate to God personally, but I must also relate to him as part of that body. That is something many of us don't know how to do.

Think of the church as a choir. Fifteen or thirty or fifty individuals are singing. They have individually given of their time and effort to prepare and present this anthem. But I shouldn't hear fifteen or thirty or fifty individual voices. I should hear one voice, a blend of all voices.

This picture of a choir gives us several exciting applications. Consider this: You have probably heard choirs that featured one superb soprano and a number of other so-so singers. The soprano's voice sticks out. You come away saying, "She had a great voice," but the overall presentation was not inspiring. Actually, it might have been better if she had not been singing. The resulting blend of average voices might have created a much better sound.

A choir is not the sum of its voices. You might say it is the "product" of its voices. The choir's quality cannot be measured by the combined quality of all its singers; it is rather the way the voices work together. This is true even in the physical structure of music. Two notes, sung in perfect harmony, can actually produce a third note (which is the difference in their frequencies).

You find the same thing in the theater. When casting a play, I'm not necessarily looking for the actor with the best skills of speaking and moving. I want the actor who knows how to give, how to relate to other characters. I don't want people walking away saying how great the actors were—I want them to be touched by the play.

152

As you look around, you will see examples of this everywhere. The best volleyball players I know are not the spikers but those who have a good team concept. They can spike, but they also can set up the ball for others to spike. They move to cover the gaps in the floor; they know what the team needs to win.

It all comes back to Paul's body analogy. We can't all be eyes and ears. Some of us are feet and arms. But we all work together to serve the Lord.

We tend to think of the worship service as the collection of each one's individual worship experience. Picture it as a wire extending from each worshiper's head into heaven. Along this wire we send our praises and receive our blessings. We take care (well, some of us take care) not to disturb or distract anyone else—we mustn't get those wires tangled. Each Sunday hundreds of wires rise to heaven from our church.

When we come together as a church body, something else is going on. Something greater. Let me suggest that we wrap the wires together, that we weave them into a huge, thick rope. Suddenly I'm not sure where my strand ends and where another's begins, but I know that I am part of that rope that reaches to God. I am joining in the corporate worship of my church. Together, we are a unit. We are more than the sum of our parts. We are a body, connected to each other.

Two attitudes make this work: submission and a Greek idea we'll borrow again from the early church, *homothumadon,* "same passion."

Submission. Back in college, my theater group played a game that illustrates this point perfectly. We all closed our eyes and started moving slowly through the room. Our theater was a large storeroom in a dormitory basement—good room to move, but you had to watch out for pillars. There would be twenty-five or thirty of us moving slowly through the room. When we bumped into another person, we were cemented. We had to keep moving, but now we moved together. We would bump into another, and then three of us would move, and then four. Ultimately, the whole group would be joined—and we would still be moving. Our movement was the combined force and direction of everyone in the group. Each one of us contributed to the group's movement, although no single one of us had originally intended to move in this direction at this speed. If I knew more about physics, I might explain it in terms of vectors. Each of us was moving in a certain direction with a certain force, but when we merged with another direction and another force, we would have to adapt.

153

The church is like that. One person wants more hymns, another more preaching. One wants to get rid of the announcements, another wants to be sure Awana activities are mentioned. One wants more classical music, another wants simple choruses. Each person pushes in his direction with a certain force. Compromises are reached. The church keeps moving.

Church leaders try to keep everybody happy. They usually just keep everybody equally unhappy. People are just satisfied enough so they don't leave the church, but they can complain. And they do.

What's the problem? "I can't worship with those songs! I don't think it's proper to do that. It hampers my worship experience."

As long as we continue to think of our services as mere collections of individual worship experiences—the many wires—the complainer has a point. But if all of us can see our worship as a combined activity, a celebration of our church's relationship with God, then we can all rejoice. The complainer can see how he or she has contributed to the style of the service, even though every detail may not be exactly to his or her liking. And the complainer can rejoice in the gifts of other people, as well. The complainer needs to submit his or her own preferences to this wonderful sense of participation in a diverse group of believers.

Imagine a choir where Barney Bass sings a booming chorus of "How Great Thou Art" while Tony Tenor pipes in with "Christ for Me," Suzy Soprano does an aria from "Messiah," and Alice Alto does the descant from "It Is Well with My Soul." And the whole time the director is trying to lead a Gregorian chant.

All the singers may sing marvelously. Every note (except for a few high G's in "Christ for Me") is perfect. But the result is horrendous. They must cooperate. They must sing with each other.

But Barney Bass can't stand operatic arias, and Suzy Soprano sneers at silly choruses like "Christ for Me." Alice won't do anything that doesn't have an alto descant. And the director wrote this particular Gregorian chant, so she feels quite strongly about it. Unless someone submits, there will be no harmony. Some compromise has to be reached. Maybe one style one week, then another. Maybe another style altogether. Maybe the director will impose her will on the rest. But they all must agree to sing whatever they decide to sing—and sing it joyfully.

"Submit to one another," Paul wrote, "out of reverence for Christ" (Eph. 5:21). When we think of submission, we usually think of leadership. It may surprise you that in these paragraphs on submission, I haven't said anything about submitting to the pastor or elders or worship leaders. There is a place for that, but the submission I'm talking about is more along the lines of Paul's words—"submitting to each other." In this matter of worship styles and preferences, even leaders need to submit to the Spirit's working through the church.

We give God worship from what we have, from who we are. These are our firstfruits we give. We can't just borrow a bushel from the guy down the block. God wants *our* souls in worship. Each church has a certain identity. The gifts and goals and desires of each church flow together in different ways. The leader must be aware of that as he plans the worship services and leads them.

Homothumadon is the word used frequently in the early chapters of Acts to describe the church acting "together." That is how the New International Version usually translates it, but the sense of the word goes deeper. Literally it means "like-passioned, having the same inner feelings." And the word's use in Greek literature as well as Acts indicates that *homothumadon* does not have to mean utter unanimity in all things. In some cases there are people with serious differences who unite in a particular matter because they share a common goal.

That brings us to our worship services. We are not cookie-cutter people. We have differences. We may have serious differences about how to worship God. But we share a deep desire to worship God. We share a love for the Lord. So we can put aside our differences and worship together.

Easier said than done.

Those differences are often deep-rooted. But I think the key goes back to the direction of our worship. Worship is for God, you recall. That enables me to submit to my brother or sister and join together in presenting something that I may not be crazy about myself. But God has asked me to submit, and he has asked me to worship, and I believe his Spirit is flowing through my brothers and sisters as well as through me—so I can trust that God accepts this gift of worship and likes it. Even though it may leave me cold.

A man in my church used to sing in nightclubs years ago. Now he sings in church. But he still has that "nightclub" style. He has a lovely voice, but he is a crooner. And in my musical purism, I didn't like it when he sang. It wasn't my style. It made me think of Frank Sinatra, not Jesus.

Most of the people in my church thought he was the greatest singer since David. And I admit this made me a bit jealous. You see, I sing in church, too. My style is, well, I keep trying to do Christian rock, but it always comes out kind of folksy. I know my style is not the favorite style of most of the church people, but they say nice things to me anyway.

As the years went by, I got to know this "nightclub singer" a little better. And I slowly realized: That was his gift. He knew how to croon. He was deeply in love with the Lord and was giving God the best that he had. Who was I to disparage it?

My gift was Christian rock. And even though people may not have enjoyed the style, they supported me because they knew I was giving a gift with all my heart to God. Why couldn't I do the same with this other singer?

Something changed in my heart. The jealousy went away. And I began to truly enjoy his music. When he sings, I join in the worship of God—because he is a member of this body and he is giving a gift wholeheartedly to God. We share a *homothumadon,* a common spirit. I can say amen—yes, Lord, that's my gift, too. That's our gift as a congregation.

Sociologists have observed that people tend to gather with others who are like them. This has led some church growth experts to propound the "Homogenous Unit Principle"—essentially that the fastest and easiest way to grow a church is to focus on one particular social group.

I've always had problems with that. I don't doubt the validity of the scientific observation or the integrity of the principle's proponents. But Christ breaks down social barriers. In the early church, as today, Christ brings together rich and poor, educated and uneducated, different races.

As long as we come to church as consumers, intending to receive individual blessings from God through the "show" that is put on—the Homogenous Unit Principle works. We will attract people who respond to that style of presentation.

But if our churches redirect their worship toward God—and if they begin to recognize their own identity as groups, not just individual worshipers—we will break down the barriers. Because even if I don't share race, economic class, or education with the person next to me, we do have in common the most important thing—a passion to worship our Lord.

EIGHTEEN
WORSHIP INVOLVES THE WHOLE PERSON: BODY, MIND, AND EMOTIONS

Let's say you are sitting alone in a church pew, reading your Bible and praying. Through the miracle of time travel, some biblical person—say, Luke—walks in and asks you what you are doing.

"I'm worshiping," you say.

The good doctor looks at you a bit funny. "No, what are you doing right now?"

"I'm just sitting here reading Scripture—in fact, something you wrote—and meditating on the Lord," you reply. "Like I said, I'm worshiping."

"No, you're not," he answers. "You're just sitting there."

Obviously we have a problem of definitions. In the biblical languages, worshiping always meant doing something. People moved when they worshiped.

We see this in the language itself. The Greek word with the Bible uses most often for worship, *proskuneo*, literally means "to bow down before." You remember those many passages in the Gospels where people knelt before Jesus and "worshiped" him.

But there were also many other physical expressions of worship. The Psalms regularly depict the raising of hands in worship, a custom that apparently remained into New Testament times, since Paul tells Timothy, "I want men everywhere to lift up holy hands in prayer" (1 Tim. 2:8).

"Clap your hands, all you nations," a psalmist said, "shout to God with cries of joy" (Ps. 47:1).

David even danced before the Lord "with all his might" (2 Sam. 6:14). And the very last psalm calls God's people to "praise him with tambourine and dancing" (Ps. 150:4).

But this sitting down and quietly "worshiping" would seem strange to the biblical writers. Yes, they did have times of quiet meditation. Those can be wonderful times of "meeting with God." But, especially in corporate worship, the Bible is awash with physical celebration.

So why are we so sedentary?

We come to church, find a seat, sit. We stand to sing, we sit. We stand to sing, we sit. We stand for the benediction. We leave. Not exactly the Richard Simmons' Workout.

Evangelicals have always been more concerned with internals than externals. This is healthy, for the most part. We have seen meaningless physical rituals in other traditions and have determined not to be caught up in them. We have cultivated the spiritual life of the heart and mind. We don't need the physical forms, we say. Those are just on the outside. The important interaction with God happens on the inside. That is where we will do our exercises.

We have placed the cautions of the prophets over the exuberance of the Psalms. The prophets warned against actions of worship that were only external, so we have swung to the other extreme, making our worship only internal.

We have also bought into a kind of "neo-Gnosticism." Actually, that term can mean a million things in this New Age era, so I had better define it. I'm referring to the Gnostic heresy that afflicted the early church. One of its assumptions was that the body was evil, or at least unimportant. The spirit was good. Many modern Christians have unwittingly adopted this belief. We have misunderstood Paul's teaching on "spirit" and "flesh." We have taken this to mean that anything physical, any emphasis on the body, any physical pleasure, is bad.

Paul was not saying that. "Flesh," in his writings, means our physical desires apart from the control of God's Spirit. "Spirit," of course, indicates God's Spirit controlling our physical lives. Our bodies, when motivated by God's Spirit, are not bad at all. They are temples of God's Spirit. They are servants of God's will.

Like the prophets, Paul railed against a Judaism that was all flesh and no spirit. People observed the physical rituals but had no underlying relationship with God. The answer is not to do away with physical worship, but to fill our physical worship with God's Spirit. We need to let God's Spirit enliven our bodies to worship him fully.

Warren Wiersbe wrote:

> There is a strange attitude in the evangelical world that moves people almost to delight in opposing and even destroying the beautiful and the artistic. This attitude is born of a false dichotomy that is unbiblical in its divorcing of "matter" and "spirit." The advocates of this approach tell us that God is concerned with the soul and not the body, and that the spiritual is far more important than the material.
>
> This philosophy is destroyed by one great event: the Incarnation. If matter is evil, or is not important, why did God become man? If we are to focus only on the invisible, why did God become visible? . . . A beautiful building or statue or song can glorify God and bear witness to him just as much as a devout prayer or a fine sermon.[1]

We are in danger of making the "Malachi mistake." The people of Malachi's time offered God second-rate worship; God felt cheated. Now, they had some spiritual problems that we may not have. They offered shoddy worship because God wasn't very important to them. God is important to us, but our sedentary, nonphysical worship makes it look as if we don't care. Malachi's words make it clear that God wants both the internal and external worship. He wants hearts that care enough to present full, let-out-the-stops praise. He wants people to be so crazy about him that they won't worry about looking "undignified." He wants us to forget our hang-ups and send him our affection as fully as we can. We need to let our deep feelings of joy and love and repentance and praise come out through our bodies.

Someone has likened worship to a kiss. If a husband and wife do not kiss each other, something's wrong with that relationship. They may feel all sorts of emotional love for each other. They may say they love each other. They may even do some errands for each other, such as taking out the garbage. They may go out to dinner together. But if they never kiss, something is wrong.

Now the kiss in itself is very little. When you begin to analyze it, it seems silly. "A kiss is just a kiss." But in the context of a genuine loving situation, it is essential.

So it is with worship. We can feel infatuated with God. We can tell him we love him. We can even do loving deeds for him, cleaning out the garbage from our lives, taking poor people out to dinner. But when we don't worship him in physical ways as he asks us to, something's wrong. When we ignore Communion, baptism, kneeling, singing, processions, clapping, dancing, bowing—the relationship is not whole.

These actions in themselves—as with the kiss—may seem silly. Bread and wine are just bread and wine. But in the context of a genuine loving relationship with the Lord, the physicalities are rich with meaning.

Certainly, a kiss does not make a strong relationship. There are some great kissers who are lousy spouses. So, going through the motions of worship, without living a life of commitment to God, is meaningless, empty. But we must learn this point: To have a heart full of love for God, but to prevent that love from motivating the body into actions of worship, is also incomplete.

This word we have been following—*proskuneo*, worship—comes from two shorter Greek words: the prefix *pros*, "before, in front of"; and *kuneo*, "to kiss."

"Kiss the Son, lest he be angry" (Ps. 2:12).

Jesus pinpointed the Great Commandment of the law: "Love the Lord your God with all your heart and with all your soul and with all your mind and with all your strength" (Mark 12:30). Jesus was quoting from the *Shema*, a text from Deuteronomy 6 used regularly in Jewish worship. Deuteronomy mentions only heart, soul, and strength. Jesus adds *mind* in Mark's account, but in Matthew he kept *mind* and dropped *strength*. These differences may just reflect different Jewish traditions. Through the centuries, the Jews would have understood the main force of the commandment to be: Love the Lord with all of who you are. As they became aware of different aspects of their personality, they may have introduced different words to express the totality of human interaction with God.

If we choose to distinguish, *strength* certainly refers to our physical being; *mind* is our intellectual capacities; *heart* may be the human will or perhaps that part of us that responds uniquely to God; *soul* (*psyche* in the Greek) probably indicates our emotions.

Surely we are emotional beings. And if we are to love the Lord with all we have—then our emotions are part of the package. But just how much of the package should they be?

160

An interesting controversy is developing within evangelical worship on this very point. Many evangelicals are discovering emotional worship. It has long been the province of Pentecostals and charismatics. We expected "them" to jump and holler and cry and get all caught up in their emotional love for the Lord. But we suspected that they were weak on the intellectual understanding of Christianity.

I still remember an interview in the *Wittenburg Door* about a decade ago in which the wife and cohost of a Pentecostal TV preacher reportedly said, "It feels so good to be a Christian that, even if it weren't true, I'd still believe it." It has taken me ten years and I'm still sorting through the logic of that statement. By now, that preacher has been disgraced, his wife publicly maligned. And I wonder if it still "feels so good" to be a Christian. When the hard times come and the feelings fade, is there a faith to fall back on?

We mustn't judge all Pentecostals or charismatics by that infamous couple. I merely mention that to indicate how non-Pentecostals have perceived the emotionalism of the Pentecostal tradition. While we would have to admit that there was nothing wrong per se in responding emotionally to God, we have generally believed that time would be better spent in serious Scripture study rather than all that hootin' and hollerin'.

My friend Linda Richardson has been, with her husband, Bill, a significant shaper of my own thoughts on worship. She wrote to me about her background and awakening:

> My whole adult life has been filled with an almost total emphasis on Christianity as a head trip. The alliterated ditty "Fact-Faith-Feeling" was drummed into my head over and over. The facts were the important thing. Our faith was in the facts and whether or not feelings followed was inconsequential. . . .
>
> The total reason for going to church, according to our brand of the gospel, was to hear the preaching of the Word. . . . It seemed that all was geared to the proclaiming of the Word. If there were songs or offerings or special music or Scripture readings, it all seemed to be used to fill time just until we could get to the real reason we were there—the sermon—which gave us the facts. . . .
>
> The Spirit's ministry was rarely mentioned, and if there was any teaching on the Holy Spirit, it was always carefully insulated with "Fact-Faith-Feeling." "You can't trust your feelings!

Don't worry if you don't feel anything. That is not important. Facts don't change; feelings do." At that point I took great comfort in those statements. I knew all the facts but felt very little.

An encounter with God at age twenty-six changed that for me. All of a sudden I was filled with feelings . . . love, awe, admiration, wonder, a beginning appreciation of who God is . . . and I believe for the first time I began to worship. . . .

And so, here I was, filled with new feelings with no way to adequately express them to the Lord. . . . I was being told that these feelings were "froth, unreliable, and temporary" at best and "dangerous, over-emotional, fanatical and heretical" at worst.

Examination of Scripture told me that loving the Lord with heart, mind, soul, and strength must include emotions. Mary's response to Jesus in breaking the alabaster box of ointment and anointing him was extreme and emotional, and yet Jesus' words were very positive: "This will be a memorial to her."

Like Linda, many evangelicals are now rethinking the role of emotions in worship. They are waking up their worship services and unleashing their deep feelings for God. This gives them great freedom and a feeling of exhilaration. They have liberated themselves to truly "rejoice in the Lord."

Other Christians, however, are afraid that this new emphasis on emotional worship will draw attention away from God and toward our own feelings. I have articulated some of these concerns in chapter 15, "Worship Is for God."

We need to cut through this carefully. We mustn't stifle our emotions. We must worship God with our whole selves, emotions included. As John MacArthur has said, "Worship is all that we are, reacting to all that God is."[2] God does bless us as we bless him. We should enjoy the "worship experience."

But whatever "emotional high" we get should be rooted in God's expression of himself. And it should be directed back to him. It is very easy to get caught up in the music, the hype, the fuzzy feelings of a worship service, and forget who it is we worship. As Anne Ortlund has written, "It isn't the 'worship' you're to worship."[3] Yet many of us can begin to do just that—worship the worship service—unless we regularly redirect our worship to God.

162

I mentioned "fuzzy feelings." I do not mean that all feelings are fuzzy. I mean feelings that spin off from other feelings which spin off from other feelings. Let me explain.

In his book *Worship,* John Piper made a big point of the fact that emotions are "ends in themselves."[4] That is, you don't feel something in order to make something else happen. You just feel. But let me add that emotions are not "beginnings in themselves." They don't just happen; they are caused. They are responses to other things.

In worship, it is important for us to respond to God with our emotions—not just to respond to other emotions. God reveals himself in many ways to us: through his Word, through the church body, through his Spirit's whispers in our hearts. We should respond freely with emotions of joy, love, and conviction. These feelings, rooted in God's revelation of himself, are not fuzzy at all. The Fact-Faith-Feeling image does work, but it is not some train where the caboose is an afterthought. The three belong together. If we feel nothing in response to God's revelation, then maybe we don't understand the facts right, or maybe we don't believe them.

There is something to be said for balance. We should be worshiping God with body, mind, and emotions. Historically, different Christian groups have slid off this merry-go-round in one direction or another. Catholics have tended to emphasize the physical forms of worship and have often neglected the inner emotional aspect. The Pentecostal-charismatic movement has emphasized emotions and body, but in many cases it has neglected the mental aspect of worship. They need to hear Paul's cautions in 1 Corinthians 14—it is the intelligible, proclaimed witness to Christ that convinces the visitor that "God is really among you!" But evangelicals, by and large, have emphasized the mind and neglected both the emotional feelings of worship and the physical forms that should express them.

Notes

1. Warren W. Wiersbe, *Real Worship* (Nashville: Oliver-Nelson, 1986), 130-1.
2. John MacArthur, quoted in *Focal Point,* published by Denver Seminary, Oct.-Dec., 1984.
3. Anne Ortlund, *Up with Worship* (Glendale, Calif.: Regal, 1975), 64-5.
4. John Piper, *Desiring God: Meditations of a Christian Hedonist* (Portland, Oreg.: Multnomah, 1987).

NINETEEN

WORSHIP INVOLVES PREACHING AND LISTENING

I went through a stage of wondering how important the sermon was in a worship service. There is enough singing and speaking and praying and standing and walking and eating and drinking and baptizing to do—who needs a sermon? So I thought.

But then I read Nehemiah 8. It seems Ezra the priest read the law from dawn till noon one day to some of the Israelites who had returned to Jerusalem from captivity in Babylon. The people stood to hear the Word. Ezra read. Ezra blessed the Lord. The people said, "Amen, Amen," lifting up their hands. Then the people bowed their heads and worshiped the Lord with their faces to the ground. Then the Levites began to read the law and explain it to the people.

The people, hearing the demands of the law, were sorrowful. But the Levites said, "This day is holy to the LORD. Do not mourn or weep. Go home and celebrate."

The Word of God—in both its reading and its explanation—was central to that worship service. Note that the "preaching" of the Levites in this case had two functions.

First, it was a matter of *bridging a cultural gap*. The people of Ezra's time probably spoke Aramaic, a derivative of Hebrew, but significantly different. The Scriptures that they had were written in old Hebrew—which would be hard for most of the people to understand.

A modern parallel might be the King James Version, which is unintelligible for many modern readers. Or perhaps we need to go back farther, to the Old English of *Beowulf* for a suitable comparison. Whatever, the people's language had changed. They needed the Levites to explain what the law meant.

Second, the Levites *suggested an appropriate response*. The people had a natural reaction of grief over their failure to follow God's ways for all these years. The Levites in this case had to cheer them up, to remind them that God could still do great things with them, to send them home rejoicing in their newfound faith.

Today, the ministry of preaching has these same two aspects. The preacher bridges the cultural gap between the world of the Bible and the modern world. This is done by acquainting the listeners with the ancient culture or by rephrasing the ancient words in modern contexts. We need to know what the Scriptures meant to the original hearers and how that translates into our terms today.

The preacher also suggests appropriate responses. Many call this "application." The Scriptures need to make a difference in our lives. We need to know how we should live differently in response to God's Word. The preacher, moved by God's Spirit, gives us that direction.

Much has been written about preaching and teaching. Are they the same thing? I don't think so. I think preaching encompasses teaching, but it includes more. These two aspects of preaching from Nehemiah 8 support this idea. The first aspect, bridging the cultural gap, is very much a teaching thing. The preacher needs to relate the facts of the ancient world, the meaning of words, and the interplay of various Scriptures. He needs to impart knowledge to his hearers in order to bridge that gap.

But the second aspect, the response area, seems to go beyond that. It is not just imparting knowledge, but moving the soul. The Holy Spirit moves in a special way through this aspect of preaching to guide and direct Christians.

The Holy Spirit is the Counselor, who comes alongside us and says, "Here is how to live." How does the Spirit speak to us? Through visions? Sometimes. Through a still, small voice? Yes. But very often through the explanation of Scripture. The Spirit whisked Philip away to the Gaza Strip to explain Isaiah to a puzzled Ethiopian (Acts 8:26-40). The Spirit told Ananias to be ready when Saul needed an explanation of his strange vision (Acts 9:1-19). The Spirit prompted Priscilla and Aquila to explain to Apollos about Jesus (Acts 18:26). In fact, the proclamation of the early church—Peter, John, Paul, Stephen—was almost always explanation of Jewish Scriptures. These preachers explained God's Word in the light of Christ and suggested the response of commitment to Jesus.

This second aspect of preaching is what Paul called "prophesying" in 1 Corinthians. It is not necessarily a matter of predicting future events, but it does look forward. It says, "This is what you need to do in the future to please God." It is not necessarily a "miraculous" occurrence, but it is a gift of the Spirit. Prophesying is always based on God's Word, centered on Jesus, and for the good of the church.

I knew a very humble pastor who wondered why he should preach. "Who am I?" he asked. "What wisdom do I have to impart to these people? Wouldn't it be better just to spend that half hour reading Scripture to them? Doesn't God say things better than I could?"

Yes, God does say things better, but he speaks through pastors. The pastors are not (or should not be) imparting their own wisdom but delivering the message of God to their churches. If we were just people of the Word, we would be satisfied with the mere reading of Scripture—and perhaps some teaching. But we are also people of the Spirit, people of redeemed lives, who apply the teachings of God's Word to our lives in fresh ways each day. Therefore we need the ministry of prophesying as well, to move us to live as God intends.

The ministry of preaching has its counterpart: the service of listening. "When I declare the Word of God I offer sacrifice," said Martin Luther. "When you hear the Word of God with all your heart, you are offering sacrifice."[1] Scripture is full of exhortations to hear the Word of God. This is just as much an act of worship as preaching is.

"Hear, O Israel: The LORD our God, the LORD is one" (Deut. 6:4).

"Speak, LORD, for your servant is listening" (1 Sam. 3:9).

"He who has an ear, let him hear what the Spirit says to the churches" (Rev. 2:7).

Worship is a response to God. In order for us to respond appropriately, we need to hear accurately. In order to praise God for his greatness, we need to hear how great he is.

If I am acting in a play and someone comes up later saying how great I was, I appreciate it. "Which part did you like best?" I might ask. If my admirer hems and haws and says, "Well, I don't know. I really wasn't paying much attention," the praise loses its validity. So with God, we need to *hear* his revelation of himself in order to know how to worship him properly.

Hearing is also an act of submission. If I were to interview, say, Billy Graham, I would spend most of my time listening. I respect him; I think he has a lot of valuable things to say, so I would keep quiet and learn from him. My attentive silence indicates, "What you say is more important than what I would say." And so it is with God. We don't want to enter the divine presence yakking away. We want to hear the great, life-changing things he has to tell us.

Hearing also leads to obedience. In fact, in Hebrew the word "to hear" often means "to obey." It was assumed that full attention to God's Word would result in obedience.

A nagging spouse might say, "I told you so—but you wouldn't listen." He or she is not just talking about hearing, but about taking the advice, doing what was said. The biblical words have the same sense. Jeremiah complains about his people: "They did not listen or pay attention; instead, they followed the stubborn inclinations of their evil hearts" (Jer. 7:24).

When we truly listen to God's words in worship, they will change us.

> As the rain and the snow come down from heaven, and do not return to it without watering the earth and making it bud and flourish, so that it yields seed for the sower and bread for the eater, so is my word that goes out from my mouth: It will not return to me empty, but will accomplish what I desire and achieve the purpose for which I sent it. (Isa. 55:10-11)

Notes
1. Warren W. Wiersbe, *Real Worship* (Nashville: Oliver-Nelson, 1986).

TWENTY

FOUR WORDS OF WORSHIP: HOLY, HOSANNA, HALLELUJAH, AMEN

Worship starts with a vision of God's holiness. Isaiah saw God high and lifted up, and angels singing, "Holy, holy, holy." John saw a similar vision in Revelation.

Holy is related to the word *whole*. That makes sense. We human beings are lacking something. We are not whole. Something has been wrenched from us. Some life-giving elixir, some sense of Eden. We wander this world in search of that missing ingredient that will make us complete.

God has what we lack. He is complete. He is holy. As we catch a glimpse of his perfection, we realize that only through connection with him can we be whole. And yet, with Isaiah, we bemoan our own unworthiness. The holy God is wholly unapproachable—unless he can cleanse our sin.

Our recognition of God's holiness makes us exalt him with great praise, but also bow in confession before him. He is worthy. We are not.

We line the streets as the holy king approaches. We sing his praises as we crane our necks to see him through the crowd.

We expect him to ride a white warhorse up the temple steps and take his throne. He will oust the usurpers and judge the world in righteousness. Once again, the world will function as it ought. He will lead us back to Eden.

We join our voices with the innocent children, but we know that our hearts are dark. We long to ride with the King as he establishes his kingdom, but we know we don't deserve to be near him.

But look! The King rides, not on a magnificent stallion, but on a pitiful donkey. He is dressed as we are. He is one of us. He will not shrink from me as I approach him. He will not sneer at the stains on my garment. He will not mock my dark heart.

The children wave palm branches and the people are forming a carpet with their robes. The King rides toward his kingdom amid the worshipful cries of his people. I raise my voice, too.

"Hosanna!" I cry. "Lord, save us."

I pull off my tattered robe and lay it at his feet. It is unworthy, I am unworthy, but I know he wants it. I know he wants me.

"Lord, save me!" I cry as he rides by. He is my only hope.

The King meets me in that moment. His gaze meets mine and burns away my darkness. He fills my soul with light. As Isaiah's lips were purged by the burning coal of God's holiness, so my soul is touched as he assures me that his death will make me clean.

White-robed, I join the multitude before God's throne. The final victory has been won. The tumult is past, the kingdom is fully here.

The King ascends his throne, but not in flowing robes. He wears the wool of a lamb, a constant reminder that his sacrificial blood has brought us here.

As we see him, the crowd erupts with one accord in a word of praise, "Hallelujah! Praise to our God!"

The angels bid us to join the wedding feast. The Lamb is the happy groom, the host of this reception. But where is the bride?

We are the bride. We, the multitude of believers, look down at our white robes and understand. He has clothed us. Once unworthy of his holiness, we are now invited into his family, onto his throne. He asks us to share this festive banquet with him.

"Hallelujah!" we sing again, praising not only out of awe and respect but out of deep love. Our God is great—and he's ours.

He speaks and we listen. He shares with us the wonders of creation. We see our world with new eyes. He speaks with deep wisdom and helps us understand his mysteries. We keep thinking the honeymoon should be over, but it keeps going on and on. We bask in his presence.

He asks us to speak, and we do. Miraculously our feeble words become eloquent in his presence. He who turned water into wine is changing our stutters to songs. It is beyond anything we could ask or even think. It is great to be with him.

"Amen," we say. "Yes, let it be, Lord, as you want it to be. Your kingdom come, your will be done." Our moments of worship now are but a taste of that eternal companionship. We enjoy it now and long for the future fullness.

"Amen. Come, Lord Jesus."

These four words—*Holy, Hosanna, Hallelujah,* and *Amen*—give us a simple pattern for our worship.

Holy—we recognize his holiness and greatness and praise him for it; we confess our own unworthiness.

Hosanna—we recognize our dependence on him to save us, perhaps reciting a creed of the basics of our faith; we make our requests, asking him to intercede in our world for the sick, the troubled, the oppressed.

Hallelujah—we rehearse the wonders of the salvation he has provided and we praise him; we thank him for specific victories he has won in our lives.

Amen—we hear his Word and utter our agreement; we commit ourselves to obey what he says.

TWENTY-ONE
FORMS OF WORSHIP SHOULD BE APPROPRIATE TO THE SPIRITUAL REALITIES THEY EMBODY

We have been looking at scriptural principles of worship—big, broad themes that you can apply in many ways. We've been dodging many of the questions that have been dogging you readers. Things like:

Should the choir wear robes?

What color?

Where in the service can we put the announcements without ruining the mood?

Should the choir sing Bach cantatas or John W. Peterson cantatas or some of these Maranatha creations?

What can we do about that really nice tenor in the choir who can't sing?

Drums in the sanctuary?

Dare we raise our hands in worship? What will everyone else think?

I know choruses are nice and all, but doesn't the overhead projector ruin the spirit of worship?

Why does that man in the back pew shout amen so much?

Should we use unleavened bread or Wonder Bread for Communion?

Should we put a Christmas tree in the sanctuary?

Why do men always hunch over like that when they pray?

These are the questions that try our souls. Sometimes they split churches. Relax; I will still dodge these questions, but I'll offer a principle that may help you deal with them.

The forms of worship should be appropriate to the spiritual realities they embody.

The actions we do in worship mean things. They express what is going on in our souls. We should choose the actions that give best expression to what is happening inside us.

In my church, we stand to sing hymns. Why? I don't know. It could be that, in offering praise, we stand in tribute. It is sort of a standing ovation for the Lord. It might also be that standing helps us sing better, and we want to give God the best music possible. Once, someone on a worship committee with me suggested that we stand during the hymn right before the offering so that the men could dig the wallets out of their pockets more easily. This is probably not the best reason. It has some practical merit, but it has little to do with the spiritual realities of singing praise to God.

We dress up for church because it is appropriate to present our best to God. Yet some Sunday, if the theme is repentance, people might be invited to attend in their "grubbies." Bluejeans and sweatshirts might be a modern equivalent of sackcloth and ashes. (The Chapel of the Air designed a program that involved "bridging the gap between church and your daily work." One Sunday it was suggested that people come to church in their working clothes, whatever they may be. This was an appropriate way of bridging that gap, symbolically committing to the Lord their weekday lives.)

When we pray in church, men "hunch over like that" because they're bowing. That is an appropriate posture in which to address the sovereign God. In some churches people kneel. This is also appropriate, probably more so.

A friend of mine told about a meeting he had with an African Christian. After they talked, they decided to pray together. My friend, a Conservative Baptist, bowed his head reverently. The African stretched out on the floor, prostrate before the Lord. That, too, was an appropriate posture.

The choirs in many churches wear robes. In this way they indicate that they are a unit, singing together for God's glory. They do not draw attention to themselves and what they are wearing. That attention should be directed toward God.

In some churches the preacher wears a robe because he is assuming the role of God's messenger. The robe sets him apart, and yet it indicates that he himself is not the special one. It is the gift God has given and the role he has assigned that makes him worth listening to.

I have heard several different pastors puzzle over the place of announcements in the worship service. They have generally assumed that announcements spoil the mood of worship. The usual solution is to put them at the beginning, before the "worship" starts, and get them over with.

I disagree with that whole line of thinking. Worship is not a mood we need to drum up and maintain. It is a meeting with God. Part of that corporate meeting can involve a celebration of who we are as his body and how we are involved in serving him. The announcements can even be seen as a presentation to God of our weekday lives. As such, they fit very nicely with the offering or pastoral prayer.

We should affirm all appropriate choices, even while seeking the most appropriate.

It's Mother's Day. The four-year-old announces that he has a present for Mommy. Eagerly he runs to his room and gets it. When he returns, she closes her eyes and holds out her hand and receives her gift. It is a rock.

What does she do? She thanks him and hugs him and listens to him tell how it was the nicest rock in the whole yard. It is a wonderful gift because it came from a loving heart. That makes it appropriate. Maybe flowers or jewelry would have been more appropriate, but the rock is great.

So it is with our worship. As we ask these tough questions about "appropriateness," we can get very picky. In our desire to find the most appropriate forms of worship, we can begin to put down forms that are less appropriate but well-meant. We shouldn't let this happen.

God heard the prayer of the African who lay prostrate, but he also listened to my friend who bowed. There was nothing wrong about that bow, even though the lying down might have given fuller expression to the inner sense of humility before God. We should encourage each other to worship God as fully as possible, but we should do so with much love.

Different churches may have slightly different spiritual realities. I'm a Baptist. I think the Baptist form of baptism by immersion is very appropriate. It beautifully depicts the act of dying with Christ, being buried, and rising with him.

But I won't crow about that before my Presbyterian friends because it really doesn't apply. Their baptism of infants by sprinkling symbolizes a very different spiritual reality. It depicts the conferring of a covenant, and it mirrors the Jewish rite of circumcision.

I had a Presbyterian girlfriend who came to my Baptist church and was appalled by the song leader. This was something I had grown up with—somebody comes to the pulpit, announces the hymn and its number in the hymnal, and sometimes even waves his arms to direct the congregation in singing the song. She thought it was very undignified, inappropriate for church. Yet I found her church very stiff. The organ starts to play. The numbers are posted on a board up front. People stand when the pastor stands. And they sing. All very dignified, but it lacked the vibrancy and personality that I liked.

I could go on and on about the appropriateness of one church member summoning the rest of the church body to join him in singing praise to God. But she could answer with a stirring defense of the need for reverence before our great God. The fact is that our hymn-singing styles reflect two very different spiritual realities—both of which belong in the church.

So, once again, keep your eye out for more appropriate forms, but don't be too quick to judge others.

There are always practical considerations. We have imperfect bodies in an imperfect world. We will always be limited in the forms of worship we can choose. Maybe you believe in the appropriateness of the choir wearing robes, but your church can't afford them. Maybe you would like to urge your congregation to kneel in prayer, but most of the parishioners are elderly and would find it rather painful. Maybe you would like the choir to sing the "Hallelujah Chorus" every Sunday, but they just can't handle it. Maybe you would like to worship "in the round" to indicate that we are all the "performers" and God is our audience—but the building is set up differently.

There are people-practicalities, too. Sometimes trying to push some new worship form on a congregation would cause more trouble than it is worth. A worship dance, for instance, might be a great way to honor God, but it might distract some worshipers.

Be sensitive to the practicalities, and be sensitive to the people in the church, but beware of granting anyone absolute veto power. "We've always done it like this" is not a good enough reason to keep you from seeking a more appropriate form. "That's too Catholic" or "That's too Pentecostal" shouldn't be roadblocks for you either.

Then again, "All the churches are trying this" may not be the best reason for you to try something. Keep looking at appropriateness. How well does the physical form express the spiritual reality?

In the first worship committee I was involved with, Sterling Nelson was the voice of practicality. The chairman of the church board, he had a deep love for the Lord and a desire to worship him fully. But he also knew the logistics of a worship service. He knew what would distract and what would offend.

Pastor Bill Richardson and his wife, Linda, and I would go crazy with our ideas of how to worship each Sunday. Let's try this. How about this? We relied on Sterling to tell us what would work. Once he said, "You have to change something. You have the people standing for the first half hour." We had been perfectly justified in having the people stand for this hymn, this prayer, this anthem, this reading—but Sterling knew that people's feet got tired, and people with tired feet can lose their focus on God. Time after time, he tempered our plans. He never dowsed them. He had a good heart for worship and came up with great ideas of his own, but he made sure that our ideas never ran too far ahead of the congregation.

We wound up planning some creative worship services, but nothing shocking. It was not a case of a handful of visionaries alienating the rest of the church. The congregation was with us each step of the way. We learned to worship together. And all because Sterling kept us aware of the practicalities.

I want to suggest three areas of appropriateness that can strengthen many churches' worship services.

1. *Participation of the body.* The structure of most worship services plays into the mistaken assumption that the leaders perform while the people watch. The early church wasn't like that. The "snapshots" we have show us a multigifted congregation in which many people ministered.

Since we are the body of Christ, given various gifts for the service of God and each other, we should open up our services to participation by many members. Choirs are great, but let us involve people in Scripture reading teams and drama groups as well. Let us allow people to voice their prayers or stand up and launch their praises.

2. *New songs.* The Psalms often direct us to "Sing to the LORD a new song." Many of us like the old songs too much.

Actually, the old favorites are fine. Those very psalms became old favorites that were sung by the early church. But the church also writes new hymns, and it has done so through the ages. Today there is an exciting supply of new hymns and choruses. We should use these to praise our Lord in fresh words and tunes.

177

It is appropriate to sing new songs because we are new creatures. The Spirit blows through our lives afresh each day, showing us new mercies every morning. Our hearts should be inventing new ways to praise God.

Encourage the creative people in the church to write new songs, dramas, and special readings. These will not be as familiar or beloved as the old classics, but they should reflect the living power of God's Spirit at work in your congregation.

3. *Amen.* Black churches are known for their amen-saying. The people urge the pastor on with "Amen! That's right, preach it!" We should all adopt more of this attitude and use more of this word.

Amen signals our agreement with what is being said or done. It also signals our participation.

I was visiting my parents once when Mom announced she was sending a wedding gift to friends of our family. "Do you want me to sign your name to it, too?" she asked.

When I said yes, I was participating in the offering of a gift. Mom had bought it and wrapped it, but because of my family connection with her, she was inviting me to be included as a cogiver. That is what happens when we say amen.

A soloist sings a lovely song. It is a beautiful gift to the Lord, prepared and presented by the singer. But because I am a fellow church member, she invites me (and the others) to "sign the card," to make it our gift to God, too. When we say amen, we participate in the giving of that gift of worship.

Amen-saying may enliven the church's worship, but that is not why we do it. We do it because it is appropriate. We serve a God who utters truth and invites our participation with him through his Son, Jesus. We say yes to his truth and to his invitation. "For no matter how many promises God has made, they are 'Yes' in Christ. And so through him the 'Amen' is spoken by us to the glory of God" (2 Cor. 1:20).

TWENTY-TWO

EPILOGUE: ONE CHURCH'S PROGRESSION

We were in the Stupe, the college snack bar, where we all did our best thinking. Al was the assistant pastor at a struggling church. Jana and I helped him lead the youth group.

Al was always finding fascinating things in Scripture, things that matched our church's situation perfectly. He would expound them with such conviction that we loved to listen to him, even when we didn't know what he was talking about.

Jana was finishing a dish of mint chocolate-chip ice cream, I was slurping a soda, and swirls of steam rose from the coffee cup next to Al's open Bible. He had found a gem in John 17, Jesus' prayer for his disciples.

"Jesus prayed first for their relationship with God," Al explained. "Then for their relationship with each other. And finally for their witness in the world. Why do you think he does that?"

Al was always asking questions like that. He was born to be a professor or a philosopher. We knew that if we kept quiet long enough he would eventually give us the answer.

"Does that order tell us anything about the church?" he added.

"I bet it does," I volunteered. "What do you think, Jana?"

"Sounds good to me," she answered, as she gathered the last bit of ice cream in her spoon.

Al smiled at our mockery and sipped his coffee. "These, ladies and gentlemen, are the biblical priorities for the church. Number one—

relationship to God. This happens individually through salvation and personal commitment, but how does it happen corporately?"

"Worship," I answered.

Al gave me a great look, half-surprised that I had been paying attention. "Number two," he continued, "relationship to each other."

"Fellowship," said Jana.

"Right again. And number three—witness to the world?"

Jana and I said it in unison: "Evangelism."

Al grinned as if he had just completed a doctoral dissertation. "Ah, yes. And there you have it."

"What?" I wondered.

"The three biblical priorities for the church: worship, fellowship, evangelism."

"In that order?" asked Jana.

"That's the order in which Jesus prayed."

"But it's hard to build a case on that alone," I said. "Look, I agree with you, but you're not going to convince anybody on the basis of John 17."

"Are you really saying," Jana paused for a moment. "Are you really saying that worship is more important than evangelism?"

Al thought for a moment. "More important among equals, I'd say. They're all important. But when Jesus prayed for his disciples, what does he seem to be most concerned about? Their relationship with God. And what did he say was the greatest commandment in the law?"

"Love the Lord your God with—"

"Exactly! And what was the second?"

Jana answered slowly, as if the idea were catching fire in her brain. "Love your neighbor as yourself."

"Is the one more important than the other?" Al asked. He was on a roll now.

"Yes and no," I replied. "Both are important, but one comes first."

Al was furiously flipping through his Bible now. "And what does it say in Galatians—let's see, where is that?"

It was my turn to shine. "Galatians 6:10, Do good unto all men, especially to those of the household of faith,'" I quoted.

Amazed, Al and Jana stared at me. I shrugged. "I memorized it in junior high Sunday school."

Jana was putting it together. "So we're supposed to love all our neighbors, but especially our fellow believers."

"Ah, yes. But does that diminish our love for nonbelievers?" Al asked.

"It can't. It all has to be there," I answered. "But—but how does that work in the church? How do you 'prioritize' three things you're always supposed to be doing?"

"I think it works like this," said Al. He was about to be prophetic. "You know how much our church is struggling right now. We really haven't been very effective in evangelism. It looks like we're good in fellowship, but think about it. Who fellowships? People who already know each other. The older people talk with each other, the middle-aged people talk with each other, the younger people—"

"We don't have many younger people left," quipped Jana.

"And here we all are," I said, raising my soda in a cynical toast.

"You see, that's not really fellowship. Well, it's not the ideal. It's friendship, it's social interaction. There's nothing wrong with it, but— it's just lacking something."

"If we were to focus on worshiping God, if we were to come to grips with who we are as a church in relationship to God and learn to celebrate that on Sunday morning—things might be different."

"Do you think that would enhance fellowship?" I asked.

"I think it might. You see, we wouldn't be just friends, we'd be co-worshipers. We would care for each other in Christ."

"And that would flow out in evangelism," Jana suggested.

"It would have to. There's nothing more attractive to the unbeliever than a caring, worshiping community. I really think the best avenue to church growth—which everyone in the church wants—is not some evangelistic campaign, not some dynamic preacher, but worship, which leads to fellowship, which leads to evangelism."

I left the Stupe with a new concept of the church's agenda. It all made sense to me.

Our church was in the throes of a virtual church split. The pastor had been asked to leave a year earlier, and a number of the younger families of the church had drifted away. I remembered when 200–250 people had crowded into the sanctuary for Sunday morning worship. Now we were fortunate to draw 80. We were not at all close to finding a new pastor.

Al was busy behind the scenes caring for people. The youth group had dwindled, but we kept doing fun things. He also tried to shore up the damage. He would meet with departing members, sometimes trying to woo them back to our church, but always making sure they had moved to some good church.

Six months later, Al left. There was no money to pay him anymore, and not enough people for him to minister to. I found myself assuming more and more responsibility at the church—we had a huge organizational structure and few to fill the positions. Choir director, Sunday school superintendent, deacon of Christian education. And then I was teaching an adult Sunday school class. My topic: "Three Biblical Priorities: Worship, Fellowship, Evangelism."

We hardly got past worship. My "students" were enthusiastic, and I kept learning new things about worship in my research. Much of the material in this book was born in that class.

The church got a new pastor that spring, after two and a half years without. Bill and his wife, Linda, came to my class a few times and were eager to work with me in planning the church's worship. We formed a worship committee—the pastor and his wife, the board chairman and his wife, and me. Later, Jana joined the committee, then others. We met each week to plan the Sunday service. Later, there were two committees, planning alternate weeks.

That time was precious to me. We tried some new things in worship, we kept some old things. We learned a lot. The church surprised me with its readiness—I had expected more resistance. Not that we were running roughshod over everything they held dear, but the church members were mostly middle-aged and older and I guess I thought they would be more stodgy. I grew much closer to many of these people—my co-worshipers—in that time.

Six months later, I moved away. Of course, the emphasis on worship went on without me. Bill and Linda continued to research, to explore, to experiment, along with the worship committees. About once a year I would have occasion to travel back to that area on business, and I made sure to stop in at the church. These occasional "checkups" thrilled me, as I saw the church growing in many ways. I would also meet with Bill and Linda when I visited, and they would fill me in on what was happening. I draw my observations from these conversations and my sporadic glimpses of the church in action over these last nine years.

I wish I could say that the church was packed the first time I returned. No, it was still drawing about eighty to the Sunday morning service. But in those early years there was a growing excitement about worship. Sunday morning was a celebration. More and more people used their gifts in the service. Some led choruses, some read Scripture, some sang or played instruments, some gave testimonies about the Lord's activity in their lives, some prayed, some had made banners that hung on the front wall. In general, I noticed much more music in the service and much more Scripture reading. I would come away from these services with the distinct impression, deep in my soul, that the Lord was pleased—and that pleased me.

At about year three or four I noticed something else. It seemed that there was more attention to the needs of people in the congregation. The pastoral prayers were long and earnest, and there was more intercessory prayer from the congregation. One church member had cancer, and church people rushed to support her however they could. A church family lost their teenage daughter in a car accident, and the church grieved together.

As I talked with Bill and Linda in these "middle years," they were speaking less about the new things they were attempting in the worship service and more about the needs of church people—and how the church was banding together to help.

This was true fellowship. Oh, I'm sure there was still socializing along the usual lines of age and life-stage. But I was hearing about people of different ages caring for each other, praying for each other. They were co-worshipers, brothers and sisters in Christ.

The church numbers were growing, despite some setbacks. They lost some key members due to retirement and job transfers, but they crossed the one-hundred mark by attracting a number of new young families. Even this, however, was not the ideal kind of "church growth." It was the migration of the saints, Christians leaving one church and finding a better home in another. Some of these were Christians who had moved into the area. There were few new believers in the ranks.

But around year six, things were changing further. Attendance was pushing 130, and there were many new faces I didn't recognize in the service. Bill and Linda were talking now about this family and that family—they weren't Christians yet, but they had been attending and were close to making a decision for Christ. These church people had started a Bible study and invited their neighbors. Someone else had been bringing friends to church. They had to hold a baptismal service for the first time in years. They weren't sure if the faucets still worked.

This was church growth the right way, welcoming people into the kingdom. Evangelism was happening, not through special programs (though they were planning some), but through the personal contact of vibrant believers. These believers were bringing their friends to a worshiping, fellowshipping community.

On my next visit I sat in on the last session of a Sunday school class that had focused on ministering to the needy. Apparently the class had covered scriptural exhortations to reach out in Christian love to needy people in the world. In this last session, one of the class members asked, "What now? We've covered the need for us to minister. What are we going to do about it?" They decided they could form a "Good Samaritan" committee (Baptists are always forming committees, but this one would work) to investigate needs in the community and in the greater Chicago area and plan ways of meeting them. In that class the groundwork was laid for a committee that actually was formed and is now moving quickly (sometimes so quickly that the board gets worried) to scout out needs and offer assistance.

So here we have a church that is effectively—not perfectly, but effectively—evangelizing and meeting physical needs in the community. Al told us it would happen like this.

It took almost a decade for this church to reach this point. That may seem like a long time. Of course this church was in sad shape when the process started. It might not take a healthier church quite as long to go through this cycle.

It should be said that this church was not neglecting fellowship or evangelism during those years. It held plenty of church suppers and gave much to missions. The emphasis on worship never implied, "Do not fellowship. Do not evangelize." In fact, I think there was always a sense that those other aspects were the proper outgrowth of worship. I remember a powerful sermon Bill gave at a missions conference during his first year at the church. "God seeks people to worship him," he quoted from John 4. "Worship leads to evangelism, and evangelism leads to worship."

But what is most striking about my church's story is that the impetus grew from the inside, from the hearts of the people. There was never really a master plan: We'll do worship for three years and then fellowship. There was just the initial focus: We need to learn to worship God; we'll see where he leads us from there. And he has led, not only the church leaders, but the church people. Bill and Linda weren't orchestrating the move into fellowship and evangelism—they were watching it happen. And when was the last time you were in a

Sunday school class where the students, not the teacher, said, "OK, we've learned this. Now what are we going to do about it?"

There are things you do because you're told to, and things you do because you want to. A child might be told to clean his room. He might do so grudgingly, or, if his favorite uncle was visiting, he might do so eagerly.

We Christians have been told to worship God, to care for each other, and to minister to the world. My church could have focused first on ministry to the world. It would have planned door-to-door canvassing, evangelistic rallies, fund drives for Christian charities, etc. But why? I suspect the motivation would have been like that of the kid who was told to clean his room. We want to be obedient, so we do it.

Now there is nothing wrong with obedience; it's wonderful. But it is so much better when our hearts are in it. Leaders know that evangelistic campaigns can be like pulling teeth when people's hearts are not there. The people need to be reminded over and over, "God wants us to do this." Often Christian leaders speak of evangelism in assembly-line terms: We win new believers and make them soul-winners to win other new believers, etc. But why?

The biblical priorities make sense because they carry our hearts along with the heart of God. He wants us to love him and to show our love, not only through individual holiness and devotion, but also in corporate times of celebration and commitment. This love spills over to our fellow believers first in acts of caring and fellowship. Then the love keeps spilling outward. God wants others to worship him, too, so we invite others to join us. We want to reach out to others out of love for God and others, not only out of a sense of obedience. This energizes our evangelism and public ministry from within. It makes it a passion, not just a project.

I don't know what lies ahead for my church. They have faced some difficulties, they may face more. Maybe they will come full circle in a few years and return to a new emphasis on worship. Maybe this book will need a sequel.

But a theory has been borne out. It may not work this way for every church, but it has some biblical basis. And undoubtedly, in the study of his Pennsylvania church, Al is sipping his coffee as he reads this and saying, "Ah, yes . . ."